Keeping Silence

Keeping Silence

Christian Practices for Entering Stillness

C. W. McPherson

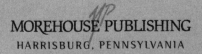

MOREHOUSE PUBLISHING
HARRISBURG, PENNSYLVANIA

Morehouse Publishing
P.O. Box 1321
Harrisburg, PA 17105

Morehouse Publishing is a division of The Morehouse Group.

The Scripture quotations contained herein are from the New Revised Standard Version Bible, copyright c 1989 by the Division of Christian Education of the National Council of Churches of Christ in the U.S.A. Used by permission. All rights reserved.

Cover design by Corey Kent

Cover art by Corey Kent

Library of Congress Cataloging-in-Publication Data
McPherson, C. W.
    Keeping silence : Christian practices for entering stillness / C.W. McPherson.
      p. cm.
Includes bibliographical references.
    ISBN 0-8192-1910-X
    1. Silence—Religious aspects—Christianity. 2. Spiritual life—Christianity. I. Title.
    BV4509.5 .M37 2002
    248.4'6—dc21

                                                                2002006721

Printed in the United States of America
      04 05 06   6 5 4 3 2

Contents

Let us do as the prophet says: "I have said: I will keep my ways so that I will not offend with my tongue. I have guarded my speech. I have held my peace and humbled myself and was silent . . ."

—*Rule of St. Benedict*

Keeping silence is all very well, but it all depends on what kind of silence you keep.

—*Samuel Beckett*

CHAPTER ONE

An Invitation to Silence

Be still, and know that I am God!
—Psalm 46:10

If I ever thought that keeping silence was easy, my congregation taught me otherwise. From time to time as a parish priest, I recommended they try spiritual practices, such as memorizing a psalm or reading the Bible daily. But one simple suggestion proved difficult or impossible for most people to follow. During Advent and Lent, I advised that they keep silence for just a few minutes each day: turn off the phone, close the door, and be silent for ten minutes. It seemed like such an easy suggestion—something people would find refreshing.

I thought wrong. Many people found the assignment impossible. I might as well have urged them to go home and memorize the Gospel of Luke.

The only people who could carry out my suggestion were those who were already used to keeping significant periods of silence in their lives. This was obviously a problem. I knew that silence was good for people. As a student of the Patristic era and the Middle

1

Ages, I had heard silence commended again and again by great voices. As a regular reader and interpreter of Scripture, I had heard the value of silence proclaimed in God's own word. I affirmed this through my own limited experience: I knew the healing and the strengthening power of silence. How could I teach the spiritual practice of silence to those who knew nothing about it? I began exploring this problem by asking people, *What's so hard about keeping quiet?*

Some people told me they were too busy to try ten minutes of silence a day. But when we discussed things a little further, we discovered that that wasn't really the problem. Their schedules—somewhat to their surprise—included plenty of free time. Others tried the practice, but they were distracted by thoughts of the urgent things they should be doing. Some said it just felt empty, like a dead and futile silence. Others admitted that silence frightened them, or that it hurt them to keep silence. It hurt some people physically: They itched, they ached. Some it hurt psychologically. One person told me it "just reminded her of everything that's wrong." They found, in short, that when exterior noise was removed or diminished, interior noise took over, which was uncomfortable. An exercise intended to be meditative was, for many, stressful instead.

And so they gave up. My suggestion to keep silence as a way to simplify life, to find calm, to get relief from the stresses of a busy world, only augmented their stresses. Replacing external noise with inner noise was a poor bargain, for the inner chaos was worse than external agitation. As so many have told me, "It sounded like a good idea, but then I tried it."

I thought long and hard about this. Why should something that a few people find so pleasant be so painful to others? And why should something so simple be so difficult? I began to realize how alien silence has become for so many of us. Noise is now natural to us, while silence is strange and foreign. We have come to accept the current noise level as part of the natural order of things, even though it isn't. It is a product of the mechanized world, and that world is, on the time scale of history, still very new. From a historical perspective, the sort of noise we have grown used to is quite abnormal.

Our forebears lived in a much quieter world. Consider this: Until about two hundred years ago, the loudest sounds many people ever heard were thunder, church bells, and the occasional rifle. The nineteenth century brought factory sounds, combustion engines, telephone, and railroad noise into human life. And the twentieth century brought us heavy machinery, the sounds of amplified music, office machines, domestic gadgetry, television, radio, computer, and compact disc. Globalization, moreover, has managed to distribute the problem to very nearly every part of the world. Electricity, the transistor, and the computer have brought amplified noise into the domestic lives of peoples who were virtually untouched by Western culture just decades ago. We speak blithely of a "global village," but it might be more accurate, psychically and physiologically, to speak of a global "big city" because the smallest hamlet today has access to the noise levels of Times Square, while Times Square has absorbed very little of the placidity of a tiny hamlet.

We are subjected to an intensity and consistency of noise that is absolutely unprecedented in human experience, and we often don't even take note of it. The loud sounds that scared us as little children now scarcely catch our attention. I can remember being frightened by the noise at the railway station when I was a small child. Today, I scarcely notice the stupefying noise of airport travel.

If you don't believe me, let me suggest a simple experiment. Right now, close your eyes and listen. What do you hear? Unless you happen to be on some sort of retreat, or live in an unusually rural place, you will hear several of the things I have mentioned. Do you hear traffic sounds? Electric gadgets? Television, radio, or some other electronic medium of communication and entertainment? Computers? Machinery? Heating or air-conditioning? Spend at least two minutes making a mental list of the things you hear at this moment. Now imagine that number multiplied by a factor of about 5,000. This is the amount of noise you endure every day.

For practical reasons, we usually do not notice most of the noise. Our consciousness works by filtering and skipping, admitting only the noises we need to heed deliberately. Parents of young children know this phenomenon well: They can ignore the sound of a crowd, even a crowd of children, but will immediately attend to the sound of their own child's voice. But we hear noise, even if we do not notice it. We get used to it by becoming somewhat oblivious to its presence. As a result, silence now seems abnormal. Remove the envelope of noise and we become anxious and nervous. Just as a long-term prisoner, released from jail, finds freedom confining and longs for the regularity and predictability of life on the cell block, we long for what we know: noise. Our noisy world acts as a kind of insulation, a distraction from the serious concerns that silence often invites.

That's one reason many people resist even the possibility of silence. The Stoic philosopher Seneca complained about the noisy business of his world—the Roman Empire—and maintained that serious thought is only possible in silent retreat. But back then, as now, many people find such serious thought unwelcome. Silence reminds us of ultimate questions, of life and death, of meaning, of finitude. Many of these are issues that people prefer, consciously or unconsciously, to avoid. Perhaps in part because it prompts us to face uncomfortable truths, silence has certain negative connotations.

Silence is a natural symbol for death itself, as in the phrase "silent as the tomb." Psalm 31 curses the wicked with silence: "Let them be silent in the grave." Silence equals death, at some level, so we are afraid of silence, as we are of death.

Silence is also associated with punishment. One of the worst forms of correction a prisoner can suffer is solitary (and therefore silent) confinement. Silence is also used to punish children. If they misbehave, they are forced to "be silent," forbidden to talk or make noise. Like the condemned person in the book of Lamentations, who has to put his "mouth to the dust" and to "sit alone in silence" (3: 29, 28), they experience silence as a punitive tool, and resent it. Actually, it may be a relatively good device, certainly better than abusive corporal punishment, but it causes some people to associate silence with wrongdoing and with pain. Being forced into silence, having it imposed in a frightening or painful way, causes people to dislike it, and to associate noise with freedom and pleasure.

Another reason we distrust silence is more positive: We really are busy people. Economic necessity, among other things, forces our busy schedules on us. Few of us have leisure to spend a lot of time in retreat, in silence. While few people today work the staggering hours most human beings suffered in earlier centuries, most of us are genuinely busy. And we have been seduced into thinking that our leisure time is best spent in being distracted: We like to "be entertained," or to "goof off."

Try this mental experiment. Walk into your nearest neighbor's house when s/he is "off," and offer them this choice: They can spend the next half hour in total silence, or the next half hour with the television turned on *at random*. Which option do you think your neighbor would choose? The tendency to avoid silence comes to the surface when we try to practice it. One of the first things we hear is a little voice that says: "You really should not be doing this. You have important things to do."

All of these factors have combined to make the simple practice of keeping silence very difficult. That problem is what prompted this book. As I talked with and worked with people in my congregation and in spiritual direction, I discovered that making a few suggestions about how to practice silence enabled them to get started. So I have put together a sampling of methods of learning silence that others, and myself, have found helpful. None of these methods are new. Many of them were used by monks, hermits, and explorers such as the Desert Fathers, far back in the earliest centuries of Christian life. The Apostolic writers, the great creative theologians of the fourth century, the medieval mystics, and various spiritual directors of the modern era all have contributed to our understanding of the practice, meaning, and value of silence; I have drawn on their theoretical and practical wisdom throughout this book.

All of these methods have been tested by busy people who lead ordinary lives. I, too, have used every technique I suggest in these pages, and every technique has also proven helpful for someone I have known either as a student, friend, teacher, or through the relationship of spiritual direction.

WHY KEEP SILENCE?

Since you are reading this, you probably have an interest in learning about the practice of keeping silence, but you may also be asking what good it will do. Why have so many explorers of the spiritual life discovered silence, then refined ways of keeping it? Why have so many ordinary people found it helpful today?

Ultimately, you will have to discover that for yourself. But let me suggest some of the benefits others have discovered. Practically everyone who has practiced silence finds that it improves concentration. Work becomes easier. Leisure activities become more enjoyable. People have told me they get more out of life simply by investing a few minutes a day in silence.

Physiologically, deliberate silence calms the body. For some people, it actually lowers blood pressure; virtually everyone finds that it steadies the heartbeat. For many, it signals the beginning of greater control over their physical lives. Bad habits become easier to discard, good ones easier to form. People involved in support groups or twelve-step groups usually find that silence helps them keep their daily resolutions. Runners and cyclists find it a welcome companion; it's a catalyst for anyone in their physical efforts.

Psychologically, its benefit lies in the balance it offers. By calming the mind, and by increasing the mind's command over the emotional life, it makes extremes easier to manage. Grief and exultation are less likely to shock and displace us.

Spiritually, it puts us in touch with reality. It makes us far more aware of ourselves, both of our souls, and our bodies. Silence returns us to the present moment, that moment we are always trying to escape. Silence is also the other—and often neglected—half of prayer. Prayer is a two-way conversation, so it must involve listening to God. And in order to listen, we must be silent. A noisy life allows us to be conscious only superficially, and a superficial consciousness excludes spirituality. Cultivating silence enables us to understand and recover our own humanity; it serves as a catalyst, bringing the presence of God into our lives and into the world.

Those who don't believe in God certainly practice silence, too. I respect the non-theistic very much, and I have profited and learned from them. In this book, however, our silence will be directed at knowing God better and listening to God more deeply in our lives.

The regular and deliberate practice of silence also teaches us a great deal about the power and importance of words. When we are comfortable with silence—that is, comfortable with not speaking all the time—we begin to choose when to speak and the words we say are said more carefully. Words become more than mere noise. Saying hurtful things, lying (even little "white lies") becomes more difficult. The torrent of words against a background of noise makes it very easy for us to suppose our words do not matter, true or false. But silence makes words stand out; their meaning resonates more powerfully. It is not at all uncommon for the practitioner of silence to discover new eloquence, new effectiveness in speaking and in writing.

Keeping silence also helps us develop empathy. The person who keeps silence regularly is far more comfortable with being quiet when another person is talking. All the well-known techniques for empathetic and effective listening—focused attention, sympathetic posture, non-verbal assent, and above all, refraining from interrupting or completing another's thoughts—come easily and naturally to the practitioner of silence. I believe this is one reason the Desert Fathers and Mothers were so often sought out for personal counseling and spiritual direction. Not only did they have choice bits of wisdom to offer; they also knew how to keep silent while troubled people spoke.

A PREFACE TO SILENCE

Let all mortal flesh keep silence.
                    —Liturgy of St. James, Hymn 324

Before you read any further, try an experiment: Be silent for just ten minutes. Insulate and isolate yourself—remove or turn off the telephone, make yourself comfortable, lock your door. Do whatever will guarantee ten minutes of quiet. Do nothing else to prepare yourself. Put nothing else on the agenda—just see what happens.

Note your thoughts and feelings during this period. You might find it helpful to jot them down for reference when the period of silence is over and as you work through the rest of this book. Note any difficulties you have, any feelings of anxiety, or feelings of absurdity. All of these are quite normal, and can be addressed easily. People who are new to intentional silence experience a bit of both. It helps to become familiar with these feelings now. The sense of anxiety will subside, but feelings of self-consciousness or absurdity are bound to recur. People who are drawn to the arts of meditation tend to be self-critical to some degree, and these feelings are simply a product of that faculty.

Of course, take note of your positive feelings: security, peacefulness, rest, and refreshment. These are not illusory benefits, and they are a welcome alternative to noise for most of us. Get acquainted with them. They are part of the reason for keeping silence, and they are immediately available.

Next, I suggest that you read through this little book quickly before you attempt any of the methods for keeping silence that I've explored. Just as you would scan a menu in a restaurant before deciding which foods you want to try, a quick preview of the book will allow you to look over the various methods, and choose one or more that seems attractive to you. Each method is put into a theological and philosophical framework—nothing too ambitious or involved, but background that will help to answer your questions.

First, a few warnings. Most people quickly discover that their own thoughts regularly interrupt their silence once external stimuli are greatly reduced. Frequently, the thought that intrudes is: "You are wasting time. You have better things to do." This is a powerful message, one that must be taken seriously if we are to make any headway. Buddhist masters have likened that thought to a monkey in the mind—it quickly takes on a life of its own, and mutates into a strangely frenetic list of things you "should" be doing—the grocery shopping, cleaning, helping the kids with their homework, and so on. Christians might think of the voice as that of Martha: She has symbolized the active life at least since the third century, when Origen of Alexandria compared Martha's action to Mary's contemplation. We tend to think of Martha's voice as a negative one, but she has her very good point to make. It's just that her timing is off. And so is the voice interrupting your silence.

The best way to handle an intrusive thought is not to resist it, but to honor it—and thereby disarm it. Treat the thought as if it were a person and say, "You are right. I am a responsible person, and you are a responsible thought. I do have things to do. And I will do them. I respect everything you stand for. But I'll take care of my responsibilities in a few minutes. What I am doing right now—or am about to do—will make me better at the very things you are reminding me to do. So just go away for the present—return later and help me meet my responsibilities then."

The trivial and the not-so-trivial thoughts will keep coming— "Wouldn't that peppermint candy taste great right now?" "I wonder how my cat is doing?" "There's a scandal at the office!"—but they can be brushed aside like flies, as contemplative masters in the East and West recommend. We only need to recognize that the busy monkey has a point to make. Give him his due, let him make that point, then put him in his place.

Secondly, as you practice silence you may discover a new and vivid awareness of your body. To some this can be surprising: After all, the body is supposed to be in repose because keeping silence seems to be a purely mental and spiritual exercise. But there is no such thing as a purely mental or spiritual exercise. More often that not we are simply unaware of our bodies: We shift our positions or move through space unintentionally. In keeping silence, many of us discover our bodies anew.

It is impossible to try to keep silence without also trying to keep still, so silence ends up being closely related to physical movement. Physicists tell us that sound is entirely a matter of motion. It is caused by the vibration, or the motion-in-place, of some material object, which sets up motion in the air, which in turn moves the membranes of the ear. Instinctively, we associate motion with sound. For example, we call a painting "noisy" if it's done in harsh, loud colors, or the design is flamboyant or intricate. We call it noisy because, even though it is mute and motionless, it makes our eyes move, it stimulates our motor imagination. It radiates kinetic energy, even though it is still.

Keeping still, physically, supports keeping silence. Try a very short experiment here: Sit perfectly still for two minutes—as still as you can. Your posture doesn't matter: Just assume whatever posture seems most conducive to stillness. You do not have to be located in a silent place, although very noisy surroundings probably will be distracting. Do this right now.

What happened? Unless you have practiced stillness through meditation, or are an especially strong-willed individual, or have an unusually centered personality, you were almost immediately drawn out of the stillness. You wanted to move. You wanted to shift positions, to rub your nose or scratch your leg; you wanted to turn your head or twist your arm. You needed to cough or clear your throat.

Even if you persevered and mastered these initial problems, you probably found yourself faced with a sudden consciousness of natural motion that you normally overlook. Your blinking eyes, for example. Or the movement of your chest and the motion of your diaphragm as you breathed. Your need to swallow at irregular intervals. Your heartbeat. You rediscover in these simple things the fact that you cannot keep literal stillness: not in the sense of an inert thing. What you strive for, physically, is the stillness of the spinning top. This is the physical counterpart to silence.

Some Basic Suggestions

In the next few chapters of this book you'll find a variety of suggestions for practicing silence. But before looking at the details of these practices, you'll need to know some basics: how to pay attention to your posture, to physical distractions, your location, and the amount of time you devote to keeping silence.

POSTURE

Almost all guides to meditation make suggestions about posture. It has always been stressed in Eastern systems, and it used to be stressed in Christianity as well. John of Damascus, an eighth-century monk, taught that a strong upright posture in prayer is a symbol of the resurrection. But for various reasons, the importance of posture has been downplayed in recent centuries. Christians have stressed the truth that "you can pray anywhere," which also seems to imply that you can pray in any position. But we have forgotten to emphasize the paradoxically complementary truth, that a stable posture and quiet body are conducive to prayer. Meditation guides in the Christian tradition, just as in Hinduism or Zen Buddhism, used to recommend a firm, well-rooted posture so that you could be motionless for a while with minimal discomfort. The most common recommendations are to kneel or to sit, either cross-legged on the floor, or in a chair. These positions encourage an upright posture with a strong spine; slumping is counterproductive.

If you normally tend to slump, at first an erect posture may seem very harsh, not at all conducive to stillness as you understand it. Although you probably recognize the need to relax during meditation, it might not seem that a strong posture is relaxing at all. Chalk this up as something new to you, for this is a truism: You cannot keep silence, in the sense we are developing here, while slumping, reclining, slouching, or any other posture we normally think of as "relaxed." Stillness involves attention, and attention is impossible when the body collapses. Relaxed postures encourage rest and sleep. These activities are vital in our lives, but they are different from attentive silence.

PHYSICAL DISTRACTIONS

No matter what position you assume at first, you will soon find yourself wanting to move. If you start with closed eyes, you will want to open them, and vice-versa. You will feel an itch or a pain. You will need to cough. Some sort of physical distraction is inevitable.

How can we move from these distractions into a state of stillness? The first step is to understand that a physical distraction is not actually a distraction. Whatever happens is exactly what you want to happen, and if it is a physical sensation, fine. The object is not to be motionless, but to learn stillness: These concepts are related, but they are not the same. When your body starts sending its signals, when your nervous system begins to buzz, understand that this is good: You are already making progress. This is supposed to happen. Many people, having heard or read about prayer or meditation and stillness, understandably assume that they are doing something wrong, or that silence is not for them, when, having settled down with the intention of silence, their body protests in this way. But you have not failed. This happens to everyone, and it never completely goes away. Be glad when the physical static starts. It means you are alive and alert.

But since these feelings are sometimes a distraction, you can learn to handle them. The most common advice is to try to ignore your need to fidget, to focus somewhere else, to relax more. Focus on your breathing, the words that constitute the subject of the meditation, the object before your eyes. Don't fight the body, but forget it. This works for some people.

Another common suggestion is to surrender, give in. If your nose itches, scratch it, if you have to fidget, fidget. Permit yourself the freedom of movement your body seems to crave. Like a small child given permission to move, your body may then give in. Readjust, then don't worry about it. A Zen master might give you different advice: Do not give in; resist. If your nose itches, if your knees ache, if your back is tired, too bad: You can stand it. Fight it. It sounds harsh and counterintuitive, since you are trying to relax, but I have seen it work remarkably well, in a large, very inexperienced group of mediators, who managed to keep silent, and amazingly still, for long periods of time. Try any or all of these strategies, and see what works best for you.

FINDING THE RIGHT PLACE

Another pragmatic concern is the setting. Where should silence be kept? There are two equally valid but radically different ways of answering this question. So different are they, in fact, that they appear at first to be contradictory. Actually, they are complementary. The first answer is "anywhere"; you don't need any special place for practicing silence. You don't even need a room that is literally silent. A noisy place can be positively supportive of silence, once you've developed the right approach. The second answer is: Silence is best practiced in a private, controlled, simple environment, reserved for this purpose only. Try to find a protected spot where you can practice silence every day—some corner of your house, some quiet room in the place where you work, a rooftop somewhere, a basement—any place that, once or twice a day, can be yours. Ideally, it should be comfortable but sparsely appointed. For example, a corner of an attic may prove preferable to a corner of the family room. When you're away from home, a dorm room or retreat cell may prove better than a hotel room. But more important here is the consistency: better a corner of your living room where you can keep quiet every day than a mountaintop retreat you can reach only once a month.

Whatever convenient place you find, make certain it is neither too cold nor too hot for you. Either can easily induce sleepiness when we work toward stillness. Also, many people feel a little colder once they keep silence, since their kinetic energy level drops. It might be a good idea to keep a blanket handy; yoga practitioners often find that helpful when they practice silent meditation after the more strenuous physical efforts of the *asanas* (yoga postures).

What about keeping silence outside? The question is often raised because it seems like a good suggestion. Experience suggests, however, that only those who normally spend a good deal of time outdoors will find this a helpful environment at first; they are used to it. For those who are not, it is too physically rugged and too visually impressive.

THE BEST TIME TO PRACTICE

What time of day is best for silence? Here again there are two valid answers. First, any time is good for meditation: You can keep silence morning, noon, and night. You can practice the art of meditation when everyone else is making noise, or when everyone else is sleeping. But at the same time there does seem to be an optimal time for the vast majority of people, and that time is early morning. This seems to work best for a variety of reasons: The mind is already rested, relaxed, and therefore more disposed toward silence. There are fewer distractions. The phone isn't ringing. Cars aren't traveling the roads. The world is quieter, cooler. All of these factors can be helpful to you when you're learning to keep silent.

PRACTICING REGULARLY

The most important consideration is the question of duration. How long should you keep quiet every day? The standard I use, and the one used in this book, is ten minutes. I base that opinion on both reason and experience. Handbooks on meditation recommend all sorts of timeframes—a half-hour per day, or two twenty-minute sessions each day—but very few people new to silence are comfortable committing that much time. Those recommendations are splendid for those who have practiced some form of meditation for many years, but for most people, such a commitment is too time-consuming, and not very appealing besides.

Most of us would be in better physical condition if we spent two hours exercising each day, and we could sharpen our wits by working puzzles an hour per day—but few of us can go to such lengths.

On the other hand, a little physical exercise is something everyone can manage; a little problem solving is appealing and practical for everybody.

The same holds true for keeping silence: a little every day is helpful for most of us, and far preferable to sporadic longer sessions. So I recommend ten minutes a day. And that is a maximum, not a minimum. Don't go beyond that, at least for a few months. When you feel as though you want to keep silence longer, you know you are making progress. Eventually, two sessions of thirty minutes will look very appealing—though you may never find that kind of time on any regular basis. Until then, err on the side of brevity and keep it to ten minutes.

Most important of all is consistency. It's all right to be somewhat flexible as to your location and posture, but here you should be most strict. Never skip a day. Even if you can only spare five minutes of silence, do the five minutes. The person who meditates for just one hour a week, spread more or less evenly over seven days, will derive more from the practice than the person who spends two hours in silence two times a week, but does no meditation on the other five days. Keep it short, but keep it daily.

Think of silence-keeping as something you "have to do," like eating or sleeping or brushing your teeth. Eventually, you'll do it without thinking much about it. That is what good habits are all about, after all.

CHAPTER TWO

Sitting Meditations

In this section, we begin to explore various techniques for cultivating silence that have been used with great success down through the ages. Although this book is not arranged progressively—no one method is necessarily any more or less difficult than any other—these initial suggestions have a certain priority for Christians. The first three have origins deep in Christian history, and the last represents a Christian borrowing of an equally ancient practice from another faith.

All involve sitting for the meditation, which most people find to be quite natural. This is the posture most of us associate with receptivity—from hours spent sitting in school, to hours spent absorbing information or entertainment as adults. Though many people also work from a sitting posture, most of us associate standing with activity, and reclining with rest. To sit is to assume the posture of comfortable attention.

Finally, although all of the ways I suggest to keep silence are simple, the sitting meditations in this section are the simplest of all. Many readers will recognize the instructions to be variations of things we normally do in informal reverie: thinking about a passage we have read, repeating some favorite line of poetry, even counting. Beyond that slight formal nudge, all you need is a quiet place to sit.

BENEDICTINE RUMINATION

Thy words were found, and I ate them, and thy words became to me a joy and the delight of my heart . . . O Lord, God of hosts.
—Jeremiah 15:16, RSV

History

Benedictine rumination, a practice for learning and absorbing the deeper meaning of Scripture, was developed in the monasteries of early medieval Europe, beginning in the sixth century. This method of meditation served the monasteries well for many centuries, and some still practice it today. The early Benedictines spent a large proportion of their day in *Opus Dei*—the "work of God," which meant worship, so they attended seven or eight worship services (called the Daily Offices) each day. Since books were rare, and most of the monks couldn't read anyway, they listened to a great deal of Scripture in the course of a day. As you might imagine, that left plenty of opportunity for distractions, daydreaming, and actually dozing off. In order to absorb the meaning of Scripture rather than simply allow it to "wash over" them, they focused on a particular verse from a psalm or some other passage of Scripture, and memorized it. They then said it over and over to themselves, extracting from it every last possible fragment of spiritual nourishment.

They compared this method to the way a cow chews its cud. Cows chew food and swallow it initially, but then they regurgitate it and chew on it repeatedly throughout the day. That allows the animal to extract additional nourishment from what it eats. Such beasts are called "ruminants." We, too, can ruminate on Scripture by hearing it and then reconsidering it throughout the day.

Practicing

I begin my suggestions for practicing silence with this practice of Benedictine rumination because it is one of the most accessible methods of meditation. During your ten minutes of silence, read over a significant passage—a parable of Jesus, say, or a story of a miracle. It should be a complete unit, yet short enough to be read aloud in a minute or two. The length of a lesson read in church is about right (scholars call this a *pericope*, meaning a "cut section").

Then, select a segment from this reading, a fragment long enough to make sense, but short enough to memorize effort-lessly—in other words, a sentence or two, or a longish phrase. For example, say you did choose one of Jesus' parables—the story of the Good Samaritan. Your segment from that story might be Jesus' summarizing question, "Which proved neighbor to the injured man?"

Now repeat your phrase or sentence. Chew on it—over and over for as long as you keep silence. You might even try doing this the way the early Benedictines did—by mouthing the words, or saying them very softly. If this is impossible or you do not like the idea, simply repeat the fragment over and over in your mind. Whichever strategy you choose, try to attend to the words and whatever thoughts they bring to mind. If you find your mind wandering to other things, simply return to your Scripture passage and begin repeating it to yourself again.

As you "ruminate" in this fashion, allow the scriptural words and thoughts to work within your mind. Let your associations and imagination flow. Free associate. Use your intellect and your memory. But keep returning to the passage itself. Do not move on to any other bits of Scripture. Let the verse center your reflections. The key to this form of meditation is to keep delving into a very short piece of Scripture for an unusually long period of time.

At first the process will seem quite familiar, since everyone has occasionally mulled over a bit of writing. But as the ten minutes ticks by, what will seem odd is the extent of the process. Few people who have not practiced meditation will have focused so single-mindedly for ten minutes on a single passage.

But you can even go beyond the ten minutes if you like. You can do what the Benedictines did, and make this meditation part of your whole day. Begin your day by meditating on the passage, and then continue to focus on it as you can until bedtime. Or, if you do your ten minutes' meditation at the end of the day, recall your passage the next morning and carry it with you until evening. Try to memorize the passage, if you can. If you find that difficult, write it down and slip it in your pocket or bag. That way, should you forget the exact wording, you can retrieve it. Recall the verse throughout the day. Use it to sanctify a period of waiting while you're in line at the grocery store or the bank. Use it whenever you travel if you can do so safely. (Reading Scripture while driving is not recommended.) Return to the meditation before meals, or at any other convenient moment. Call it to mind deliberately, at least five times during the day, and keep repeating it to yourself.

This method provides a simple structure that may help you practice silence and take it with you through your day, particularly if you are new to keeping silence. Like the Benedictines, who carried their bit of Scripture out of the chapel and into the fields, take your verses with you as a souvenir of silence, to savor as you please, whenever and wherever.

Another byproduct of this approach to silence is that by returning to your short passage throughout the day, you'll find yourself memorizing the passage without consciously trying to do so. As you mentally "chew" on it, you'll find yourself discovering depths and subtleties in the verse, connections that you have never made before, even if you are very familiar with the passage. When meditating in this deceptively simple fashion, people often discover new meanings in Bible verses they learned as small children and thought they had exhausted. Even biblical scholars who have approached Scripture in depth find that Benedictine rumination can reveal new insights they had not gleaned from study alone. A final blessing this method often provides is the sense of integrity it gives to your day.

Many people experience the lapse of the day's hours passively: They rush to get a certain number of things done, but they don't experience the day as an integral unit. Returning throughout the day to a simple meditation gives a profound integration to the day—and to you. It brings the day full circle; returning to the verse you started with that morning brings a sense of completion and satisfaction.

This practice is a simple and basic one, a good starting place for many. It may be one you want to stay with for quite a long time, or return to regularly. The single drawback to Benedictine rumination is that it involves so many words. When we make keeping silence our aim in meditation, even a short passage may, at some later point, begin to seem too "noisy." In fact, all the verbal methods share this drawback. They are great catalysts for keeping still, but they do fall short of pure silence. If you find, after one week or more, that you crave a deeper silence, I invite you to try the method in the next section, which is practically wordless. But if this method suits you, by all means stay with it. It was, after all, the way of St. Bernard, one of our spiritual giants, who meditated throughout his life.

Another version of this kind of meditation uses larger portions of Scripture—perhaps a whole story. For example, consider the story of Jesus' visit with Mary and Martha (Luke 10: 38–42). Benedictine rumination might seize upon the single verse, "Mary has chosen the better part," and repeat that throughout the day, mulling over the meaning of the words. Following this second method, you would consider the entire passage: the story of Jesus' visit, the actions of the two women, the words of Martha, Jesus' rebuttal; the context; echoes and parallels elsewhere in Scripture and beyond; its meaning, rationally considered; its emotional effect; its moral application; its theological implications; its lessons for spirituality; its history in Christian thought and doctrine, and so on.

This sounds, at first, more difficult than focusing on a short phrase. In fact, it is not. It is simply more complex, and surprisingly, complexity in spiritual matters actually can be easier. It is like the difference between examining a single brush stroke and examining an entire painting. For almost everyone, the latter is easier to do.

Sample Meditation

Let me illustrate this method by using an example from Luke 18:13. It is the story, appearing only in Luke, of the Pharisee and the tax gatherer. The passage is:

> *The tax collector stood at a distance and would not even*
> *raise his face to heaven, but beat on his breast . . .*
> —Luke 18:13, Good News Bible

Let me describe the sort of thing that can happen as you ruminate: not what should happen, or is supposed to happen, but what often does happen. First, you visualize the passage for the moment. Repeat the words *the tax collector* several times and picture him in your mind. What does he look like? Is he dressed in first-century clothing, or do you picture him in modern clothing? What is the scene in general? What buildings or structures are there? Next, you might notice the words *stood at a distance*. A distance from what? Is he at a distance from where you are? Are you in the picture at all? And what distance might that be?

Think about the tax collector's posture: He will not raise his face to heaven. What does that mean? Is heaven really "up there"? If he did look up, what would he see? Why won't he raise his face? Is he feeling shame, embarrassment, guilt, or fear? Why is he beating his breast?

You will find these thoughts occurring naturally whenever you spend some time with a passage of any length. They are the kinds of mental processes that simply seem to happen as we ruminate over a longer passage.

Then you begin to identify with the character in the passage. Again, not in a formal or deliberate way, but naturally. As you repeat the words, you feel your own way into the scene. You find yourself wondering what that feels like—to be so spiritually abject, standing before God—then you begin to feel it yourself. You search your memory, and you remember occasions when you not only knew, you felt your sinfulness. You recall the feeling of guilt, the sense of aridity and pain that goes with it. You don't just sympathize with the tax gatherer, you assume his psychological identity.

Don't stop with that. All the while, continue to ruminate on the passage—gently repeating it, again and again. It soon becomes soothing—the "confession" becomes refreshing, and you begin to sense how small it all really is—how infinitesimal your sin is contrasted with the immensity of God. It will dawn on you that countless millions have said this prayer, have followed the tax gatherer into the Temple, have felt their sinfulness and guilt as though it could stop the world, and then, with relief, realized their smallness.

You don't follow any of the steps above intentionally. Ignatian meditation, which we explore later on, makes a deliberate scheme out of these elements, but rumination simply allows them to happen. If you read these descriptions, it may seem far-fetched, but it really isn't: It happens very often when people ruminate at length on scriptural passages. The original metaphor—extracting every dram of spiritual nourishment from a passage simply by chewing it over and over—starts to make eminent sense.

PSALM REPETITION

> *For God alone my soul in silence waits.*
> —Psalm 62

History and Background

In the fourth century, John Cassian, a wandering scholar and monk, visited the Eastern desert monasteries and hermits. While there he recorded what he'd observed of these people and communities, and brought his work back to the Western Church. He was the first to mention the monastic technique of repeating psalms as a way of meditating.

Benedictine rumination may have evolved from this earlier technique; they share the element of verse. But there are significant differences. In the case of psalm meditation, the verse is obviously always taken from the Psalms. It has no larger context, either; the rest of the Psalm is forgotten. It can, of course, like the Benedictine practice, be extended throughout the day. But again, unlike the Benedictine method, which picks up new material each day, Psalm repetition can be extended for much longer periods of time. Cassian tells us that the Eastern monks who used this method might repeat a single verse for a week, or a month, or even longer. In some cases, a monk would discover a psalm that became his verse for the rest of his life.

Another difference between psalm repetition and Benedictine rumination is that this early technique involves the body with the soul in the meditation in a way that rumination does not. The Benedictines simply wanted to extract all the nourishment they could get out of a bit of Scripture. The Eastern monks wanted to let the psalm take over their souls. They wanted the psalm to become part of them, something as automatic as their breath—literally. In Western rumination, we let the mind work over the verse, thinking about it in all sorts of ways, turning it round like a jewel. The Eastern approach reverses that: You are not trying to see what you can get out of the Psalm so much as to see what the Psalm can get out of you. It is meant to work more on your unconscious mind, your body, and your soul.

Practicing

Select a psalm that you want to meditate on for your ten minutes of silence. You'll see that all psalm verses are divided into two. John Cassian recommended saying the first half of the verse on the inhalation, the second on the exhalation. Any verse of any psalm can be read in this manner: For example, here's how you would read this verse from Psalm 1:4:

The wicked are not so; [inhale]
But are like chaff that the wind drives away. [exhale]

It is simple, but highly effective. We are vitally dependent on breath. We have a certain control over it, but only so much: most of the time it is quite automatic. This method of meditating takes advantage of that, by connecting our breath with the psalm verse. Just as our breath moves oxygen throughout our bodies, breathing the psalm moves it deeper and deeper into our souls.

John Cassian noted that eventually we pass beyond the stage where the psalms seem to have their own life within us, and arrive at that place where we begin to feel as though we are composing them. We become the authors. This has to be experienced to be appreciated fully, but it happens to almost anyone who lives with a psalm in such an intimate way. Perhaps this is the key to the terrific humanity and humility of so many of those desert dwellers. They have merged with the psalms.

Sample Meditation

Psalm 55 makes an interesting choice for our practice. I choose this because it doesn't fit the popular idea of a psalm. It is one of the "complaint" psalms, which brings before God a list of grievances. Sometimes these make us uncomfortable, but we all get angry and frustrated with God and this psalm gives us an outlet for those feelings. The version below comes from the Episcopal Church's Book of Common Prayer, and includes asterisks that help you breathe the psalm. But first, just read it.

1   Hear my prayer, O God; *
    do not hide yourself from my petition.
2   Listen to me and answer me; *
    I have no peace, because of my cares.
3   I am shaken by the noise of the enemy *
    and by the pressure of the wicked;
4   For they have cast an evil spell upon me *
    and are set against me in fury.
5   My heart quakes within me, *
    and the terrors of death have fallen upon me.

6 Fear and trembling have come over me, *
   and horror overwhelms me.
7 And I said, "Oh, that I had wings like a dove! *
   I would fly away and be at rest.
8 I would flee to a far-off place *
   and make my lodging in the wilderness.
9 I would hasten to escape *
   from the stormy wind and tempest."
10 Swallow them up, O Lord;
   confound their speech; *
   for I have seen violence and strife in the city.
11 Day and night the watchmen make their rounds
   upon her walls, *
   but trouble and misery are in the midst of her.
12 There is corruption at her heart; *
   her strects are never free of oppression and deceit.
13 For had it been an adversary who taunted me,
   then I could have borne it; *
   or had it been an enemy who vaunted himself against me,
   then I could have hidden from him.
14 But it was you, a man after my own heart, *
   my companion, my own familiar friend.
15 We took sweet counsel together, *
   and walked with the throng in the house of God.
16 Let death come upon them suddenly;
   let them go down alive into the grave; *
   for wickedness is in their dwellings,
   in their very midst.
17 But I will call upon God, *
   and the Lord will deliver me.
18 In the evening, in the morning, and at noonday,
   I will complain and lament, *
   and he will hear my voice.
19 He will bring me safely back from the battle
   waged against me; *
   for there are many who fight me.

20 God, who is enthroned of old, will hear me and
    bring them down; *
    they never change; they do not fear God.
21 My companion stretched forth his hand against his comrade; *
    he has broken his covenant.
22 His speech is softer than butter, *
    but war is in his heart.
23 His words are smoother than oil, *
    but they are drawn swords.
24 Cast your burden upon the Lord,
    and he will sustain you; *
    he will never let the righteous stumble.
25 For you will bring the bloodthirsty and deceitful *
    down to the pit of destruction, O God.
26 They shall not live out half their days, *
    but I will put my trust in you.

Read through this psalm as a whole. What human feelings do you
find there? When have you felt these feelings? Paranoia, disappoint-
ment, the feeling of being persecuted and betrayed, the desire for
vengeance. The very human, natural urge toward fantasy. How
often, when we are suffering because of others, do we say some version of: "I wish I had wings like a dove," or fantasize about taking a
flight to some idyllic place? Then there is the "city." Those of us who
live in cities have probably thought: "This place where we live is rot-
ten, it has no luck, no health in it," at one time or another. Have you
ever felt the special pain of betrayal, as in v. 14? Or wished evil on
others, as in v. 16? We have been taught not to speak about such
things openly, but we have the psalm to speak them for us.

But now try praying this psalm using your breath. Try the first
verse:

Hear my prayer, O God;* (inhale)
Do not hide yourself from my petition. (exhale)

What does this verse "do"? What do you notice if you say it, not once, but as Cassian suggests, over and over in your silence? What happens when you coordinate it with your breathing, so that it begins to feel inevitable, to take on a life of its own within you?

The first verse half tells God what to do. We are used to doing this in prayer, but by repeating it, we might notice what a bold, or presumptuous or courageous, act telling God what to do really is. The second half expresses our fear that God might ignore our petition. That seems like a pretty conventional concern, something that comes up regularly in Scripture. But when we repeat it, again and again, we might start to think about the validity of that worry. When we are whiny, full of pain and complaining, people tend to turn away from us. Paradoxically, when we need most to be heard, people want to listen least. This is part of that honesty I mentioned. We really do feel and experience this, and it makes psychological sense to express it in the psalm.

As we keep repeating verses of the psalm, it might call to mind biblical stories. How often, in Scripture, does someone pray and feel he or she is not heard? Do you remember the story of the Importunate Widow, who keeps petitioning the unjust judge until he gives in to her demands (Luke 18)?

If we continue, we might think of Jesus himself, in the garden of Gethsemane, and finally on the cross, asking God why He has forsaken him. This can be a consolation for us: The God whom we approach with our complaint, perhaps a little diffidently, Jesus approached boldly, with his complaining question.

This calls to mind a particular theological concept—the *deus absconditus*, or the hidden God. How has God hidden himself from humankind? We have just lived through a century where this seems terrifyingly real. In his holocaust memoirs, Elie Wiesel regularly alludes to this theological notion: If God exists at all, God must be *absconditus*, hidden from sight. But the fact that we can and do pray the psalm, nevertheless, contains hope in it. We don't say "don't hide" to someone who already is hidden.

These are some of the associations I might bring to reading this psalm. Your own associations will probably be different. Simply listen to the words you are breathing and let them sink deeply into your mind and soul. You'll probably be surprised at how differently you hear the psalm after ten minutes of meditating on it in this fashion.

MEMORIZATION

I have laid up thy word in my heart,
that I might not sin against thee.
—Psalm 119:11, RSV

History and Background

Quickly: answer the following. What is your telephone number? Your street address? Your best friend's full name? Your Social Security number, if you are a United States citizen? The words to the Lord's Prayer?

That was easy, was it not? You were able to supply those words and numbers, probably without much thought because you had them memorized. Most people think of memorization as something old-fashioned and counter-productive. Nobody is supposed to learn "by rote" anymore. Any teacher who forces students to memorize lists of facts and figures is regarded as hopelessly out of date. But in the ancient world, the situation was very different. Books were the most technologically advanced tools for storing knowledge, and they were relatively rare and precious; generally they were owned collectively, by a synagogue, for example. Many people were illiterate, and even those who could read didn't rely on the written word the way we do, as a depository for all knowledge. They memorized what was important to them. Every bit of evidence we have from early Christian times through the Middle Ages indicates that Christians of all sorts memorized the sacred writings. Jesus himself, in all four Gospels, constantly quotes Scripture (especially psalms) with a fluency that can only come from knowing it by heart. Paul's letters are similarly full of Scriptural references, and the entire New Testament resembles a mosaic of Old Testament quotations. We can scarcely suppose all these authors "looked things up."

We find slight errors in the quotations here and there, which further suggests they quoted from memory. The very first monks took memorization even further. They sang every psalm once every single week. Inevitably, they memorized them. And since they regularly repeated the rest of Scripture as well, in most cases once a year, they memorized it, too. Even if the monks did not follow the psalm repetition outlined above, they ended up knowing the psalms by heart; many seemed to have memorized the whole Bible.

We find the same striking phenomenon when we turn to the earliest Christian writers outside the New Testament. The earliest Christian writers, the Apostolic Fathers such as Clement of Rome and Ignatius of Antioch, quote Scripture so extensively, and with such fluency, that we sense immediately that they are quoting from memory. Their frequent slight distortions of the text—irritating to modern scholars, who like word-for-word accuracy—only enhance this impression.

This sort of memorization is not just handy or impressive. The very act of memorizing is a meditative practice. When you practiced Benedictine rumination, you may have already discovered that you memorized certain passages without even trying. And in the process, you may have gained insights you otherwise would not have had.

This deeper understanding comes because memorizing, as opposed to simply becoming familiar with the text, forces us to deal with every single word and every single combination of words. We can't help but notice how they sound together, how they work together, how their meanings intertwine: In short, we comprehend the full weight of the words.

The best way to understand this is to experience it. Almost immediately, you will see what I mean.

Practicing

The kind of memorizing to start with is the kind I have already mentioned. You often have to memorize some very short bit of information—a phone number, or someone's complete name or title. Try something just a little more extensive, a little bigger: a few verses from the Gospels, or a short stanza from a psalm.

Memorize the passage you have selected. Use the same natural, simple devices for memorizing that you would use for a long telephone number: repeat it over and over, many times. Use whatever memory tricks you know: Have you ever tried to remember a new friend's name by associating the sound with other things? And do what you would do to remember a joke: note the structure, the patterns in it. You might even write it down, but tell yourself you are trying to write it in your memory; resolve to throw away the paper as soon as you can.

But don't use your usual silent time for doing this task. Do it some other time. Do it while you stand in line or are stalled in traffic, riding the train or taking a break at the office—anywhere you can squeeze in just a few moments. You might try this somewhere that seems too noisy at first: at a sports stadium or the theater. But I know it can work in these places because I do it all the time.

What happened? Were you able to memorize the lines despite the distractions? Many people are surprised to discover that they can. Memorization is actually easier for some people than either of the two kinds of meditation we've explored so far. This is a paradox we'll encounter many times. In the realm of spirituality, what is easy is not necessarily simple, and vice versa. Memorization is a bit more complicated than rumination. This makes it, for many, easier to do, perhaps because memorization requires total attention. The focus required can make it the best method for keeping silence for a person who is very distracted. I have found the practice of memorization especially helpful during busy seasons, when the work of my church threatens to erase all silence from my schedule, when the voices of responsibility, guilt, and fear try to deny silence any place in my life.

Memorization is a "strong" method; it makes more demands on our minds, and so it tends to push out other distractions very nicely. It is also more directive. It "assigns" us something definite to do, rather than simply asking us to repeat a verse or a psalm stanza. For some, that assignment makes a stronger appeal to our sense of responsibility than simple meditation. It works in our favor if we are trying to counter the secular impression that silence is not very important. We may still regard what we are doing as "nonproductive" from a business viewpoint. Yet the very act of taking a text and memorizing it "feels" important. Our inner censor may then cooperate.

As you memorize your passage, and repeat it to yourself, free associate with it, just as we did with the Psalm Repetition.

Sample Meditation

Pick a short passage of Scripture to memorize. Try Psalm 150, verses 1–6.

1   Hallelujah! Praise God in his holy temple; praise him in the firmament of his power.
2   Praise him for his mighty acts; praise him for his excellent greatness.
3   Praise him with the blast of the ram's-horn; praise him with lyre and harp.
4   Praise him with timbrel and dance; praise him with strings and pipe.
5   Praise him with resounding cymbals; praise him with loud-clanging cymbals.
6   Let everything that has breath praise the LORD. Hallelujah!
    (BCP)

As you memorized these lines, what did you find in them? For example, in order to memorize the first verse, I found myself associating and differentiating "temple" and "firmament of his power." Are these variations on the same thing, or two different things? Should I picture the Temple in Jerusalem in the first verse-half, then picture the natural heavens for the second? Or is God's "holy temple" simply "wherever God is," including that firmament? Then it occurred to me that Paul teaches us that the human body is God's holy temple: How should I work that into my grasp of these words?

These may well be the same kinds of thoughts that come to you using the first two meditative methods we've explored. It's just a different way of getting there.

THE JESUS PRAYER

The prayer will make you feel such lightness and such bliss in your heart, that you will be astonished at it yourself, and your wholesome way of life will be neither dull nor troublesome to you.
                                   —*The Way of a Pilgrim*

History and Background

We are all rhythmic creatures; rhythm is essential to biological life. Our lives are accompanied by a percussive counterpoint played by heart and lungs, beat and breath, from the moment we exit the womb until the moment we stop breathing. Our next prayer—the Jesus Prayer—is based on that fact.

The text of the Jesus Prayer comes from the prayer of the penitent tax collector in the parable we used for our Benedictine rumination. After the petitions of that self-satisfied, and probably morally unimpeachable Pharisee, the humble, and probably corrupt, tax gatherer "would not even lift his eyes to heaven, but beat his breast, saying, 'God, be merciful to me a sinner!'" This man, Jesus assured the disciples, "went down to his home justified rather than the other; for all who exalt themselves will be humbled, but all who humble themselves will be exalted." (Luke 18:14)

We don't really know how the practice of the Jesus Prayer began. Like many of the others in this book, it was developed anonymously and then was passed along in the oral tradition for years or centuries before it was written down. The practice of repeating this prayer hundreds or thousands of times per day developed over the centuries in Eastern Orthodox practice. The most famous and extensive account is *The Way of the Pilgrim*, a nineteenth-century Russian treatise that presents the spiritual adventures of a wanderer who practices this prayer. The *Pilgrim's* anonymous author suggests that this prayer began in response to St. Paul's injunction that we "pray without ceasing." My guess, however, is that this aspect of the prayer—that it seemed to answer Paul's dictum—was discovered as a kind of byproduct of a method that worked well for daily meditation.

The earliest form of the prayer, and the form the pilgrim himself is first taught, was the simple verse from Luke, cited above. At some early point, the prayer was given a christological twist. The word "God" was replaced by "Jesus," then "Jesus Christ," and eventually by "Jesus Christ, Son of God, Savior." The whole prayer then became: "Jesus Christ, Son of God, Savior, be merciful to me, a sinner," the form the pilgrim eventually learns. No one knows exactly why this development occurred. I suspect that it followed the earliest known form of the creeds, so it included a simple affirmation that Jesus was the Christ, that he was the son of God, and the savior. In that way, the prayer became a kind of creedal statement joined to an expression of penitence and a petition for mercy.

Practicing

Over the course of many centuries, the Jesus Prayer was linked to the rhythms of the body, and that's how I'm suggesting you use it. Quiet yourself for your ten minutes of silence, and repeat this prayer while breathing deeply. Pray the first part (Jesus Christ, Son of God, Savior) on an inhalation, and the second half (be merciful to me, a sinner) on an exhalation. Repeat this in a rhythmic way, relaxing and breathing deeply for ten minutes.

An even subtler way to pray the Jesus Prayer is to coordinate it with your heartbeat. We are all used to noticing our breath, at least on occasion, but we notice our heartbeat only when we are very still. Once you become aware of your heart beating, coordinate the repetition of the prayer with it. With the first three beats of your heart, say the first half of the prayer, and then say the second half with the next three beats. Eventually, the prayer will become as automatic as your pulse. As you become more practiced with this technique, you'll learn to become aware of your heartbeat and pray with its rhythm anywhere and under any circumstances. This can be particularly valuable when you need a moment of peacefulness in a stressful day.

You may find yourself uncomfortable with this prayer at first. Contemporary culture is not very comfortable with the idea of sinfulness; it is associated with neurosis and false humility. Repeating the word "sinner" makes us squirm a bit. At first there is a tendency to count our sins as we mention the word "sinner." We remember that we said something mean yesterday, that we thought something harsh just this morning. Soon, however, these thoughts are pushed to the periphery of our consciousness. The fact of our sinfulness becomes less of an issue; the focus shifts to our identity as a sinner, and we can learn to acknowledge that identity frankly. Far from a desperate self-pitying impulse, it becomes matter-of-fact, something not to worry about or even think about; we are free to confess and move on.

How can we be liberated by a prayer that says, "I am a sinner," hundreds of times? First, the prayer does not say, "I am a sinner." It simply identifies us, just as the prayer identifies Jesus. The prayer is not about the one praying, but about the one prayed to. The first half simply and fully identifies that person; the second half centers on the words "have mercy," rather than the sinner.

Second, and more important, the coordination of the prayer with the breath or heartbeat prevents any dwelling on the issue of sinfulness. The breath or pulse continues, making it impossible to stay focused on the sinfulness. There is no time for that before the next beat. The beating heart is a natural symbol of human life. To coordinate any prayer with that pulse is to give it positive connotations, to affirm it. Confessing offers an opportunity for transformation; the mercy we ask for becomes part of the act of praying.

If we use this prayer during our ten minutes of silence, coordinating it with our heartbeat, we soon experience the same kinds of oneness with the prayer that psalm repetition creates when coordinated with the breath. Of course, our heartbeat for that period will almost always be a slow, resting heartbeat. That physiological fact, combined with the meaning of the prayer, tends to have an enormously soothing and consoling quality.

If we take the suggestion of the *Pilgrim* and extend the prayer throughout the day, still coordinating it with our heartbeat, we'll experience various other nuances. When we are struggling physically or mentally, and our heartbeat becomes steady and strong, the prayer becomes insistent. When we are anxious, and our pulse races, the prayer becomes unrelenting. When we're drifting off to sleep, it becomes a sort of lullaby.

The heartbeat is even more personal, more intimate, than the breath. The heart is more mysterious: People understood the basic function of the lungs long before anyone guessed at exactly how the circulatory system worked. Virtually every human culture has, in one way or another, associated the heart with feelings. For some, this makes the Jesus Prayer too personal, too intimate. It can feel risky, an invasion of spiritual privacy. But for others, it becomes an indispensable song in the heart, a source of perpetual comfort.

THE CLOUD OF UNKNOWING: A CHRISTIAN FOCUS PRAYER

> *No one in this life, however pure, and however enraptured with contemplating and loving God, is ever without this intervening, high, and wonderful cloud.*
> —*The Cloud of Unknowing*

History and Background

The words "meditation" and "contemplation" have been used in so many ways through the centuries that it may seem rather pointless to distinguish them. But there is a strong tradition that sees meditation as the less advanced of the two. Simply put, meditation is defined as thinking about God (or any other subject), whereas contemplation is defined as the direct perception of God—the passive side of pure prayer.

This distinction has certain important implications. Anyone who wishes to make the effort can meditate, though one may have a greater natural inclination toward it than another may have. Contemplation, on the other hand, seems to be up to God. You can think about God as hard and as often as you like, but you will perceive God directly only if God lets you.

Still, there is an obvious connection between the two activities. Virtually every saint or mystic who seems to have enjoyed contemplation spent a long time preparing for it by practicing meditation. This next form of seated meditation begins to blur the line between the two experiences. It is a form of meditation designed to do exactly that—to elevate the seeker into the contemplative experience. It is an extremely advanced practice, suitable only for those who take the life of prayer with the utmost seriousness. However, I have known those who find the very series of seated meditations I have described to this point a very natural preparation for this method.

In the fourteenth century, an anonymous treatise known (to posterity) as *The Cloud of Unknowing* was written, presumably somewhere in England, apparently by a priest who served as spiritual director. It seems to have been written for a hermit or recluse of some sort, because in the prologue, the author addresses his intended reader as someone who has progressed from the ordinary Christian life through the ordered monastic life into the "Solitary." Now, the reader longs for and is ready for "perfection"—not meaning moral purity or excellence, but simply the "completion" of the task.

The title *The Cloud of Unknowing* comes from the author's theological approach. It is based on a very old Eastern tradition in theology, which now and then proved influential in the Western church as well. It is known as the *theologica negativa*, "negative theology," not because it is "negative" in any depressing sense, but because it "subtracts" all our illusory and incomplete notions of God. For example, we want to call God "good," but our idea of goodness is necessarily based on "good" people we have seen, "good" feelings we have experienced, or "good" thoughts we have had. These imperfect approximations to goodness are so limited and flawed, that we are obviously nowhere near what must be the goodness of God. We might as well forget about them, if we want the real thing. The author of *The Cloud of Unknowing* helps us learn to meditate on God by first weeding out our shopworn, cliché-ridden images and concepts, many of which we learned as young children: God as "old," God as "up there," and so on. Then we examine our more mature notions: God is "good," "forgiving," "omnipotent," and we find that these, too, are, by the strict logic of the *Cloud,* wanting. The result is a clean slate, an open and ready consciousness, a place for the real and living God to enter in. It is a somewhat painful process, but the result can be profoundly satisfying.

Practicing

The first stage of this practice is to forget everything we think we know about God, because there is only one thing we know for certain: Everything we know is incomplete and imperfect. Like Socrates, we can be sure of our ignorance. Then, we are faced with our own ignorance, our "unknowing," which looms above us like a cloud.

To pierce this cloud, the author suggests a single, focused method of prayer. In his own words, we should develop a "naked intention directed to God, and himself alone": We want direct experience of God. And we must then try to "think no other thought of him." We should not be misled by thinking about God's immensity, beauty, goodness, or any other religious-sounding concept since these concepts lead us away from, rather than toward, the real being.

This focus, of course, is supremely difficult to achieve. The author suggests that we may try a profoundly simple prayer technique. "If you want this intention summed up in a word, to retain it more easily, take a short word, preferably of one syllable, to do so. The shorter the word the better, being more like the working of the Spirit, some word like 'GOD' or 'LOVE.' Choose which you like . . . so long as it is one syllable. And fix this word fast to your heart, so that it is always there come what may . . . With this word you will hammer the cloud and the darkness above you."[1] This use of a single word for meditation has been characterized in recent decades as a kind of "Christian mantra," but there are fundamental differences between the two kinds of practices. In Hindu practice, the mantra is secret, prescribed by the guru for you and you alone; the *Cloud* asks you to select your own focus word, and makes no fuss about its secrecy. The mantra may be a nonsense word; the Christian focus word is simple and clearly understood.

The similarity between a Hindu mantra and the Christian technique lies in the way they are used. Both suggest repeating a single word, over and over. And both aim at centering the individual in the transcendent.

BREATH COUNTING

> *In the beginning God created heaven and earth. Now the earth
> was a formless void, there was darkness over the deep,
> with a divine wind sweeping over the waters.*
> —Genesis 1:1, NJB

History and Background

Christians have always borrowed terminology, ideas, and particularly spiritual practices from other faiths and more secular systems of thought. The central act of worship in the early church, the Eucharist, was largely based on Jewish table ritual, while the language of the New Testament was influenced noticeably by the philosophy of Plato, the Stoics, and other Greek philosophers. In each succeeding era, the church found things to borrow from beyond its own boundaries.

In the increasingly ecumenical world of the last century, Christians began to explore the spiritual resources of more distant religions,

---

1. *The Cloud of Unknowing,* Clifton Wolters, trans. (New York: Penguin, 1978), p. 69.

finding surprisingly compatible resources. Christians have found delightful and surprising parallels in the practices of Hinduism, the paradoxes of Zen, and the harmony of Taoism.

In recent decades, spiritual explorers such as Aelred Graham, William Johnston, and J. M. Dechanet have explicitly recommended the Eastern practice of breath counting. It began as a Yogic discipline in archaic India, then was adapted by Buddhist practitioners, and also seems to have influenced certain Muslim mystic sects.

For us, it is the logical next step in seated meditation. In a sense, it is the purest meditation we encounter. It is certainly the simplest, but paradoxically it can also prove to be the most challenging. In fact, it may be the hardest practice in this book.

Even though it's difficult, it also may prove to be the most congenial practice for some. Its Christian resonance must be experienced, rather than described, and many have claimed that this practice is a very pure, very direct path to stillness. My own suspicion is that, besides the few who have deliberately appropriated this technique from Eastern religions, many Christians down through the centuries have simply discovered it on their own, as they journeyed toward silence.

Practicing

Counting our breath as meditation draws on the skills you learned in psalm repetition. There, we used the breath to frame our short prayer, to support it and to begin to give it independent life. Breath counting simply removes the words, which helps to lead us into a state of pure meditation, focus, and calm. Beginning Hindu and Buddhist practitioners are usually instructed simply to sit in silence, and to be mindful of their breath. This mindfulness begins by counting the inhalations, slowly and deliberately.

The method is simple; you need very little instruction. It sounds easy, but you'll probably discover that it's harder than it sounds. It's the hardest of the verbal methods, and that's why I have placed it last in this section.

Try it. Isolate and insulate yourself, as described in Chapter One. Do what you can to keep from being interrupted for the next ten minutes. Now sit upright, back straight, and count your breaths, on the inhalation, one through ten (if you can get all the way to ten; if not, start over), over and over. Nothing else. As you do this, try to remain alert and attentive. You want to avoid drifting and stay focused on the here and now. You may find this concentration very difficult to achieve at first. Theologically, this trouble has to do with the Christian principle of the Incarnation—which means, among other things, that God took the here and now seriously enough to participate in it as Jesus Christ, and he found it excruciatingly difficult. Psychologically, difficulty staying focused reminds us that we constantly try to escape the here and now by all sorts of stratagems: busy schedules, daydreaming, mass entertainment, mindless pleasure, drugs, food, and, of course, noise.

Many people, having heard or read that meditation is "gentle," and that to do it you must be "relaxed," will find the strenuous work of this method confusing. You might find yourself wondering if you are doing "something wrong," or have forgotten something. The fact that breath counting is frustrating and seemingly impossible at first convinces some people that it's not for them. Know that this method is frustrating for everyone; no one finds it easy at first. Part of its value is that it teaches us patience and perseverance.

As you continue, try to breathe deeply from your diaphragm in your abdomen, rather than from your upper chest. The lower part of the abdomen actually moves when you are breathing correctly rather than the region around the heart. Physiologists have noted a correlation between our breathing and our anxiety level. When we are very anxious, we breathe high in the chest. When we feel secure and strong, we breathe low, from the abdomen. Breathe in a vigorous way, being careful to avoid panting. Breathe more deeply than usual, and more slowly, if possible. Don't force this. Over time, your breathing will slow down and deepen automatically. A breath rate of four or even two cycles per minute is not unusual. As the breath becomes stronger and more controlled, you can try coordinating your breath with your heartbeat—one inhalation per six or eight beats. Or, you can try squared breathing. Inhale, then hold your breath. Exhale, and hold your breath. Do this in a regular, rhythmic fashion, with the inhalation equal in duration to your exhalation. Yoga has several variations on these breathing practices if you want to explore them further.

Anyone who tries this method will notice several things. First, you'll become much more aware of your breathing. Most of us breathe without noticing it. We know that breathing sustains our life, but it simply proceeds without our conscious awareness. One benefit of being silent is learning to take charge of your inner life, and breath awareness is a powerful way into that process. In time, learning to take charge of your breath extends to other aspects of your inner life. You begin to become aware of your thought processes. Focusing on your breath also improves your concentration.

Some say that this method of meditating leaves out Christianity. This charge would make sense if Christianity were only a historical fact that needed words and language to keep it alive, rather than a living reality. What this method does for Christians is to refine the meditative state, which classic Christian teaching has always considered a major component of prayer life. We do not have to be speaking *to* God in order to be praying; we certainly do not have to be reminding ourselves of God's existence. We can simply listen for God's voice. For the Christian, this is what this ecumenical method invites us to do.

CHAPTER THREE

Visual Meditations

Each of the methods for meditation we have discussed so far involves sitting, repetition, and simplicity. Each also calls for the use of the auditory imagination. Whether we ruminate upon Scripture, repeat psalms, or simply count breaths, we are asked to "hear" things in our minds.

Now we turn to methods that involve the visual imagination. For many people, these may prove more effective. Our culture is profoundly visually oriented. Despite the noise level we discussed at the outset, a culture dominated in the last century by the predominately visual media of movies and television, and now by the largely visual medium of the personal computer, has conditioned us to take in information and to express ourselves in images.

For some reason, posture seems less important for these visual meditations than for the sitting meditations. These exercises can be practiced while sitting, but other postures—standing, kneeling, lying down—seem to prove equally effective. Perhaps this has to do with the very real power of the visual: We use far more nerves to see than to hear, to feel, or to taste or smell.

On the other hand, visual methods may raise some troublesome questions. A part of our Western theological heritage includes controversy about the worship of images. Particularly if you are a Protestant, you may find yourself thinking that meditating on pictures is idolatry.

That point of view deserves an answer because it raises a valid issue. There's a fine line between devotion and idolatry. But the image or symbol used in visual meditations is never an end in itself. It's always a tool to help us reach a meditative state, it's not an object of worship in itself. A few more pertinent questions are: Whom are we trying to reach? Is it a saint? In that case, are we praying to the saints instead of God?

By using visual images to aid meditation, we are far from behaving like the superstitious peasant who invokes a saint in order to have access to magical powers, who keeps a relic because it is supposed to have curative properties, or who keeps a rabbit's foot because it is supposed to be lucky.

We run the opposite risk: of failing to understand the words from the Baptismal Creed, "We believe . . . in the communion of saints." The communion we pray for in the Creed is exactly what we are trying to realize when we use any image. We are all saints in the sense the Creed intends: We are part of the body of Christ. The departed are also saints, and we depict the outstanding ones as icons. We use an icon to help us visualize our communion with St. Paul, or Mary, or whomever. We are not asking these saints for special favors, or even to intercede for us at the throne of God. We are certainly not praying *to* them, in the sense that we pray to God, confident of our access. We are very simply being with them, spending a little time with them.

If even this explanation is unacceptable to you, simply treat the icon as a reminder of the saint's life and work. Plenty of believers have used icons in exactly that way, with excellent results. Do not be surprised, however, if a sense of the reality of Paul still intrudes at some point. Icons are like that.

ICONS

*It is not divine beauty which is given form or shape, but the human
form which is rendered by the painter's brush. Therefore, if the Son of
God became man and appeared in man's nature, why should his image
not be made?*

—John of Damascus, *Defense of
Icons*, Eighth Century

History and Background

The fourth century marked the first great turning point in the history of the Christian church. For the first time, a Christian became
emperor, and the fortunes of the faith seemed to reverse overnight.
Emperor Constantine brought with him many obvious advantages—
not least of which was that Christians no longer feared being im-
prisoned or executed for their beliefs. It also brought less apparent
problems, as the multitudes now became Christian simply to be like
the emperor.

There were also changes we might label neutral, and among
these was an extensive borrowing of Roman (or Greco-Roman)
cultural elements. The vestments many clergy wear even today were
appropriated then, as were the geographical terms "diocese," "synod,"
and "province," which the church still uses. For worship, Christians
adapted the architecture of the great Roman municipal building,
the basilica. And the strong tradition of portraiture in imperial
Rome, which depicted the human face and form realistically,
became the Church's way of honoring her great heroes, her
founders, and the Lord himself.

Almost immediately, these images became a popular and powerful way of devotion. The ordinary Greek word for a picture spelled
"icon" in Roman letters, and was applied to these special pictures:
The faithful used them for inspiration to meditate on the life and
authority of the person depicted. Every church tried to own several,

and everybody wanted at least one for the home: They linked personal devotion with the public worship of the church, which was becoming increasingly grand and formal.

In the eighth century, the iconoclastic voice was raised. *Iconoclastic* means, literally, "icon-smashing," and that was exactly what some wanted to do: After all, as we have mentioned, images at first seem a violation of the Third Commandment. But an even stronger voice reminded the church of the Incarnation—Christ himself took human flesh, so there could be nothing wrong with depicting it. Besides, icons were simply too powerful to be deposed: They were in the hands and homes of the people, and so they could only be outlawed—not destroyed.

The eighth century saw the resolution of the conflict, the "legalization" of icons, and also the beginnings of a strict code for producing and using them, which applied to individuals and the church, and still applies in the Orthodox Church to this day. In a parish church, for example, a certain selection of icons always has to be displayed in a certain arrangement, reflecting the theology of the ancient church that Orthodoxy is always zealous about conserving. Likewise, strict rules govern icon production: Icons have to be made only of certain woods and created with certain paints in a certain style, then blessed with approved prayers. And, of course, the meditations used with icons also are prescribed.

Our exploration of the icon will revert to the earlier period, before these rules were fixed. Icons began simply as images; their holiness was discovered, not predetermined. People simply knew they were supposed to represent the Lord, or some other sacred person, and from there it was a matter of the heart and the eye.

Practicing

Start your own exploration this way: Before reading any further, look silently at the icon on this book's inside back cover. You can prop the book upright on a table, or secure it into position however you like; the important thing is to be able to look directly at the

image. Since the posture is much less important in visual meditations, take whatever position you would like: sit straight, kneel upright, or stand in front of the icon, if you can stand for ten minutes
without great discomfort.

Now, just gaze at it for ten minutes. Try to keep as still as you
can, as in all our previous practices, but allow your eyes to search the
image at will.

What happened? Did you find this easy or difficult? Peaceful or
confusing? Did you find a focal point or points within the icon that
kept drawing your eyes? Or did you find your gaze wandering errat-
ically all over the surface? Did you develop a sense of the icon as a
whole, or did it seem to break down into various parts? Did your
inner art critic come out? Were you wondering where the image
came from, when it was made, what it was made of, and whom,
besides the Blessed Virgin and Child, it was supposed to depict? In
using icons for practicing silence, you may find that answering
some of these questions, particularly the factual ones, helps your
mind let go of the details so you can focus on the meditation itself.

This particular icon is a very early medieval Greek-style icon of
the Virgin Mary and Child from Georgia. The two figures attend-
ing the holy pair are the archangels Michael and Gabriel. Even
though angels have no gender, traditionally they have appeared in
male form. The stoles the angels wear around their necks are those
of the deacons in the early church. Deacons were very strongly
associated with angels. The angels clutch orbs, symbolic of the cos-
mos. Jesus, too, wears a deacon's stole. In an even earlier tradition,
clearly documented in the second century, deacons were associated
with the person of Jesus. Jesus clutches a scroll in his left hand: In
late classical art, clutching a scroll was the sign of a teacher. With
his right hand he signs a blessing: His fingers actually spell, in
Greek, the words *Jesus Christ*.

The images around the damaged border are saints; to the left of
each face is the word *saint* in Greek, to the right is each saint's
name. Embossed at the bottom are the figures of Michael and

Mary again. This time, they are pictured in the earlier scene of the Annunciation, which in the first half of Christian history was far more important than Christmas.

Our reproduction is approximately one-third the actual size. It was painted in tempera, an egg yolk–based pigment: This accounts for the icon's rich yet flat surface appearance. Researchers believe the image was reworked over many centuries. They think the hands and faces belong to the earliest stratum. Metalsmiths have embellished the icon's border as well as the haloes around the heads of the principal figures.

Now return to the image as a whole. What, specifically, drew you into it? That is where the icon begins its real work. There is a gifted contemporary cartoonist, Al Hirschfeld, who specializes in theater caricatures. The essence of his remarkable talent is the depiction of a face using the fewest possible lines. Our brains seem to require very little visual information in order for us to recognize the people that we know. Something analogous to this phenomenon may explain an icon's appeal. Traditionally, icons are minimalist, especially compared to traditional Western portraiture. A few lines delineate the face; perspective and the illusion of depth are always absent since Orthodox tradition forbids the use of any sort of three-dimensional illusions. It may be hard to get used to the lack of perspective and other painting techniques of Western artists, but iconography is not about trying to discover what someone looked like. Every traditional icon is labeled with a saint's name, and thus represents someone. But this representation has little or nothing to do with historical appearance. Rather, an icon is a visual stand-in for the real person. It is like a symbolic memento of a friend.

And yet, it is more than that. Icons are anthropomorphic. They look like people, the way minimalist drawings look like people. Like the minimalist drawings, the icon is incomplete, just a suggestion. We are drawn into it because we instinctively feel the need to complete it. Marshall McLuhan pointed to this kind of artistic phenomenon forty years ago: Works of art that are minimalist, or sketchy, are more absorbing for that very reason than are detailed, perfected works. That's why icons never developed into the rich, finished paintings Western artists produced during the Renaissance.

Keeping silence in the presence of an icon leads to something surprising. After a time, the icon begins to feel real. I do not mean "seems" real, in the sense of deceiving us: An icon could never fool a sane person into thinking it was a human being. But it does, eventually, "feel" real. The closest analogy today is the computer: It absorbs so much human mental activity, and transmits so much personal information, that, after a while, a plugged-in computer becomes anthropomorphic. We "sense a living presence" in the room when the computer is on, even when it is not transmitting or receiving messages. The icon, after several weeks of silent practice, takes on much the same quality.

Here we meet with another paradox: It's the sparse, stylized icon, rather than the naturalistic Renaissance painting, that more effectively evokes the living presence of the person depicted. The painting "looks like" the individual, whereas the icon "feels like" being near him or her. This is the effect of the icon: It conveys and creates the real presence of the saint. The Orthodox Church has always argued that the two-dimensionality of icons—their flatness, their limited palette, and the various other restrictions that govern the making of icons—ensures a proper respect for their heavenly nature. The full, three-dimensional, representational art of the West is, to the Orthodox eye, presumptuous and a little blasphemous. We should approach the throne of grace with a little reverence and a little reticence, and the icon style embodies these qualities.

Finally, icons are decidedly *kenotic*, or spiritually half empty. We have to fill them in, to complete them. And to experience them, we must practice an emptiness of our own. We must divest ourselves of our normal expectations for art. The Orthodox icon provides nothing art is supposed to provide. While they often appear in museums, they weren't created for decorative display. Icons are tools for spiritual devotion and development. Because they are "pictures," most of us bring to them our expectations of pictures. Abandoning these presumptions is part of the process of encountering the icon.

Here silence is almost indispensable. Although we experience most art with a certain amount of silence, we also tend to want to talk about it, to verbalize what we see, or think we see. Before the icon, all that must go. What we see aesthetically simply doesn't matter. Our vocabulary for speaking about art has no use here. The icon is there to challenge us, to invite us into its silent presence.

The effect, when we do submit, can be almost shocking. The sense of an actual presence becomes startlingly vivid. We begin to feel "in the presence" of the person depicted. The idea is to put yourself in the person's presence, and learn from him or her.

MEDITATING ON SYMBOLS

History and Background

The first Christian art—the art of the first two centuries of the early church—was entirely symbolic. Most people didn't read in those days, and the stories and doctrines of the faith were taught using pictures and symbols. This was also a time when Christians were persecuted, and the symbols were used so Christians could secretly identify themselves to one another.

This symbolism took two forms. The first was an allegorical sort of symbolism: realistic depictions of biblical scenes, for example. At that time, artists were prohibited from depicting Jesus himself or scenes from his life—to do so was considered blasphemous. But the artist could depict a New Testament truth about Christ by using figures from the Old Testament, or by depicting one of Jesus' parables: These were indirect enough to avoid being blasphemous. If an artist wanted to express the idea of the resurrection, then he could show the three men in the lions' den, or the passage through the Red Sea, or Noah's ark: All these were symbols of the resurrection.

Artists also developed a variety of symbols, each connected to an idea they wanted to depict. An anchor stood for hope, for example, or a sword for faith. An orb was a symbol for the world. Christ himself was represented by the *Chi-Rho*, the first two letters of "Christ" in Greek. These symbols were useful precisely because they were so prevalent. Anchors and swords were common, and could be said to stand for anything; C-H-R were the first letters of hundreds of words. If the church needed to conceal things, as it did from time to time, such symbols served the purpose well.

The all-purpose Christian symbol, the fish, was very easy to hide in plain sight. And it was easy to draw: two intersecting arcs make a fish pictogram that almost anyone can identify. It had plenty of biblical resonance, especially New Testament. The first disciples Jesus called were fishermen, and the gospels generally have a maritime setting. Jesus frequently borrowed images from fishing in sayings and sermons. Beyond that, the early Christians realized that the Greek word for fish, *Ichthys*, was an anagram for the phrase, "Jesus Christ, son of God, savior."

The catacombs and other early worship sites are adorned with these symbols, and through the centuries they have become known and acceptable to virtually all Christians. Even iconoclasts accepted the nonrepresentational symbols that were closer to letters than to images. Symbols are excellent for teaching or for thinking about Christian concepts. They constitute a sort of Christian algebra and *lingua Franca*. More Christians understand the sign of the anchor or the sign of the cross than understand the word *hope* or the word *cross*. Symbols communicate with an impact and an urgency that ordinary verbal communication lacks. That's why the most important traffic signals are standard in many countries. Red lights mean stop. Because they are instantly recognizable, symbols are a very effective catalyst and focus for meditation. Because they are universal, they are easily identifiable: The anchor stands for hope, the fish for Christianity. And because they are so simple, they can easily be drawn or recognized. It takes talent and skill to create an icon, but even a child can make recognizable symbols such as a cross, sword, snake, or apple. A clumsy icon would prove very difficult to pray through, whereas a clumsy symbol makes no difference at all: that is part of its "algebraic" quality.

Symbols are also more "open" in their meaning than icons. If we have an icon of a particular saint, we naturally focus our meditation on him or her. We cannot help but think about details from the person's life, or something we infer in their personality. With symbols, we are much less directed. We can think about them historically, of course—the cross will make us think of Calvary—but we can also think about them in many other ways. We might think about its glorification, for instance, or its myriad transmutations in art. We might contemplate the fact of the intersecting horizontal and vertical lines, or about its possibilities as a symbolic glyph of the human body. Symbols are like that: They suggest, rather than define. Our meditation on them is limited only by our own imagination.

Practicing

Here is a fish.

If you like, you can enlarge it on a copy machine. Or, you can reproduce the drawing yourself: Anyone can draw a fish this way. Now position yourself as you did with the icon. Sit or stand in a way that feels strong and secure. Place the image where you can see it. Look at it for ten minutes.

I have chosen the fish, which was one of the paramount symbols in the visual language of the early church. Today it's not as well known as a Christian image, although it seems to be coming back into use. The cross, which has been the dominant symbol for centuries, is too familiar to most of us. We have a hard time escaping the established ways of thinking about it. The fish is fresher: most people know what it is, but very few have actually used one as a visual aid for prayer.

If you decide to keep silence in the presence of this symbol, you will probably find it helpful to explore the rational side first, as we did in the case of the icon. Go ahead and think about the initials involving Jesus' name and titles. Think about the significance of fish in the Old Testament, and about the role of fish in the New Testament. But then let the symbol lead you wherever it will. Do not restrict yourself to Christian or even theological realms: God created the fish. It is already sacred! Let the symbol work on your imagination and emotions as well as on your rational side.

Meditate on this symbol each day for a week. You may be surprised to discover what new associations the symbol suggests on the second day. Sometimes new thoughts occur to you after a night's sleep. But in the course of the week, don't be surprised if one day the symbol seems to offer very little new inspiration. If the symbol seems "blank" on the fifth day, simply meditate on its blankness.

Allow at least one week to determine whether symbols enhance your practice of silence. In my experience, strongly imaginative people respond best to symbols. For those who find symbols to be useful meditative tools, a favorite symbol can become the devotional aid of a lifetime. It can yield new insights and new shades of nuance indefinitely.

Here are a few other ancient and traditional symbols. You can photocopy them if you like, enlarging them to any size you want, but most people can draw them fairly easily as well. If you enjoy drawing, explore the artistic possibilities as you create your own. Even if you are just minimally handy with arts and crafts, you can make a symbol for yourself. If you'd rather buy one ready-made, religious stores usually stock attractively crafted anchors, fish, and so on, as well as all sorts of crosses. But don't buy one at first; you'll miss out on part of the experience of symbols: simplicity and availability. So learn to work with the simplest and most available of all: The ones you have right before your eyes.

CANDLE MEDITATION

As our eyes behold the Vesper light, we sing your praises, O God.
                                    —*The Phos hilaron*

History and Background

Unlike icons and symbols, candles were first used in worship for the very practical reason that people needed them in order to see. Worship in the earliest church was always held indoors, and houses in the Mediterranean world are deliberately cool and dark. Celebrants needed candles or torches to read lessons, or to read the liturgical sketches that gave them directions. And the people needed candles to keep them from stumbling.

In time, candles were also given various allegorical meanings. For the Jews, the seven-branched menorah, which originally meant "lamp stand," came to represent the seven stages of creation. And for Christians, candles came to symbolize the Trinity, the orders of angels, and so on. Nowadays, electric lights have rendered candles unnecessary for practical purposes. But the result is that for some, the allegorical importance of candles seems to have increased. Candles are also seen as a "reminder" of the ancient nature of the faith.

Why use candles if we don't need them to see? The answer is that they are somehow more appropriate to worship than electric lights. For one thing, most people love their soft glow; they find it more attractive than electric illumination. It is hard to imagine the *Phos hilaron*, the ancient candle-lighting hymn that I use as the epigraph for this section, referring to the switching on of lightbulbs.

But there is more to it than that. Candles are not only lovelier than electric light, they are also mesmerizing; they draw our attention. The flickering, fluid candle flame invites our gaze in a way that no mechanical lighting ever could. They provide a very powerful natural focus.

Candles have been used in personal devotion for centuries. In the seventeenth century, for example, when there was widespread interest in the arts of meditation throughout the Western church, many people learned to use candles as a means of keeping silence. Candles suggest the transitory nature of human life (since a candle visibly "dies" before our eyes as it burns), fragility (since they can be snuffed out in an instant), and the persistence of faith (a "candle in the darkness" is proverbial, and the fourth gospel makes it a symbol of the Incarnation). Protestant, Anglican, and Catholic writers all rang changes on these themes; poets such as Richard Crashaw and George Herbert made poetry out of such symbols.

And many people simply sat and looked at candles. Like breath counting, candle gazing is a formalized meditative practice in Hinduism, but my guess is that countless Christians have discovered it independently, as a natural, simple means for entering deep silence.

Practicing

When we discussed how to count each breath, we pointed out some surprising distinctions between "simple" and "easy." It seems like a simple task to count every inhalation, but it's not easy to do. Focusing on a single, uncomplicated object is also simple to understand, but hard to do. One item that is an exception to this rule is candles. Many people find that they're easier to focus on than other objects. Perhaps that's why candles have been a popular meditative device in Eastern religions: They are an immediate draw for so many who try to focus on them. Besides, they are cheap, plentiful, and pleasant to contemplate.

Place a candle in front of you. I suggest you place it on the floor, about five or six feet away. Most people find that's the best place for it, rather than on a table or hanging somewhere on a wall, or holding it (although once you become adept at the practice, you can do it with any candle you can see). Breathe normally, but regularly. Do not say anything in your mind. That inner silence is much, much easier to achieve while you're focusing on a candle than it is when you are counting your breaths.

Assume a firm posture: kneel upright, or sit cross-legged, or on a small stool. Unlike other visual methods we have discussed, where posture seems a little less relevant, a formal posture seems to prove very helpful when we work with candles. Perhaps a firm posture helps to balance the inherently fragile nature of candles. A strong, upright, but not rigid posture seems to facilitate this meditation very well.

Simply watch the candle and its flame. Try (gently) to let go of any feelings you associate with candles. The flame of the candle is just a focal point, nothing more. It is possible to sit or kneel in the presence of a burning candle and enjoy the beauty of the flame, but that's not the point of your meditation.

What, then, is the point? Your aim in meditation is, as always, to be silent in God's presence. See if you can "feel" your way toward this without the use of words—just be still, in the words of the psalm, and know that God is God. Do not "talk to" God or pray in the sense of saying words; just be silent, the way you might share a candlelit moment with a loved one without saying a word.

Then gradually let go not only of words, but also of thoughts. If your friend were sitting with you by candlelight, you would not "think about" your friend: You think about friends when they are absent, not when they are present. Instead, you would just enjoy the friend's presence and the candlelight. Enjoy God's presence in this way, now.

Meditating in this way with a candle is somewhat similar to the practice of counting breaths. Both are simple, minimal; both are focusing techniques. You may be tempted to combine them, but that usually doesn't work well. Breath counting involves a simple half-focused gaze, not a fixed focus like candle watching. The idea is to pay attention in order to focus your mind. Having two focal points—breathing and attentiveness—seems to defeat the purpose.

You may have discovered by now that these instructions are almost superfluous for you. Many people find candles to be self-instructive meditative tools. Unlike any of the other methods we have introduced, candles "work" for some people almost immediately; people seem to discover the technique naturally. I have never known anyone able to count breaths or ruminate on Scripture or pray with an icon without some guidance, but I have seen people sit down with a candle for the first time and begin to practice the rudiments of meditation. For such people, this seems to be an almost perfect method.

There are a few drawbacks even for this method, however. First, while candles are simple and inexpensive, you can't do a candle meditation anywhere you choose. You can practice seated verbal meditations anywhere, including public places. Candle meditations demand privacy, and that's inconvenient for those who want to practice keeping silence wherever they find themselves.

Second, as in the case of breath counting, some will object that candle watching has no specific theological content. Obviously, it's not an exclusively Christian method. Focusing on a Christian symbol or looking at an icon involves a reassuring measure of theology. Candles have no theological content. But as with breath counting, we are concerned about effectively training the spirit, not with the content of the breath or with the candle as an object in and of itself. We are studying silence here, not theology. Looking at a picture of Joseph will not teach you more about him; looking at a sword will not give you more faith. These visual images may, however, serve you well as a bridge to silence. Looking at a candle can serve in this same way.

Finally, just as with breath counting, some may find that focusing on a candle is so devoid of words and images that it's vaguely unsatisfying, even disquieting. They may simply want more content: more ideas, more words, more images, more of what feels like solid substance In fact, such people may find that every method we have described so far has been too minimalist, too empty, too impressionistic. For these people, the best route may be our next section on discursive meditation, or what has traditionally been called "mental prayer."

CHAPTER FOUR

Mental Prayer

My collegiate dictionary defines *meditate* two ways. It either means "to focus one's thought," or it means "to ponder over" some matter of thought or fact. In everyday use, the word seems to suggest a little of both. When we casually say that someone is "meditating," we usually mean that he or she is focused on some area of thought—but also that he or she is thinking it over, letting the mind range over it and explore it a bit. In everyday use, in other words, *meditate* is usually a transitive verb: We meditate "on" some thought or feeling. We do not, in everyday experience, "just meditate."

Many of our seated and visual meditative exercises progressed in exactly that direction. Ruminating on small scraps of Scripture or praying with an icon are relatively focused meditative acts.

In the early church and in the early Middle Ages, Christian meditation always seems to have had this focused character. It was, as we have noted, never without content, but that content was often limited in various ways. Even a freer method like rumination, which does encourage pondering over a particular text, is limited by the relatively small size of the text—usually just a verse or two—and by the mental act of repetition.

In the early modern era, however, a type of Christian meditation developed that was far more concerned with the "object" aspect. The ancient methods were, so to speak, stretched. Instead of taking a verse from a parable, you might take the entire story as the substance of the meditation. Instead of a psalm verse, one might consider an entire psalm.

Instead of repeating a verse, bringing your mind again and again to the same place in order to become centered, let your mind range widely, mulling over various aspects of the text (or whatever the sacred object might be). Consider it from various points of view or states of mind and feeling. This kind of meditation "thinks over" a theme, and the more completely, the better.

This technique may make mental prayer very appealing for those who find the more focused and minimalist practices a little strange and unfamiliar. Mental prayer is much more like the kind of ordinary "meditation" people naturally engage in when planning a project or solving a problem. In fact, in many ways that is what mental prayer is, but made a bit more intentional and formal.

Mental prayer differs from sitting meditations in another important way. Your posture is indispensable, of course, to a sitting meditation, and is actually part of the meditation. In Japanese disciplines such as Zen, "sitting" and "meditation" are even the same word. But in mental prayer, posture seems to be irrelevant. You can practice it while you're sitting, walking, standing, or lying down. That's one reason it's called "mental" prayer: The thinking component is so important that the body takes care of itself.

These mental prayers may be very appealing to those who find the fixed-position meditations too challenging. Some people simply find it downright unpleasant to sit during the focused task of meditation. Mental prayer may work quite well for such persons, since posture doesn't matter. Others may appreciate the flexibility of being able to practice meditation in circumstances where the formal postures aren't convenient. A busy person who wants to meditate

while riding a commuter train, for example, may find mental prayer
the perfect option.

Mental prayer is also often called *discursive meditation*, not only
because it wanders more, but also because it takes longer to do. The
classic methods developed in the early modern period were intended for people who could devote at least an hour a day to their
devotional lives. Few people have the luxury of that much time
today, which is one of the reasons I suggest you limit your daily
meditation to ten minutes.

To solve the time dilemma, think of a discursive meditation as
spread out over several days. Plan to cover the longer passage in a
week, rather than in a day. In Ignatian meditation, for example, you
could devote your ten minutes each day to a single step in the progression. Devote one day's work to the use of the imagination, for
example, or several days if you need to. If you find this method productive for you, you may want to stretch the meditation over two
weeks, or even a month. I have found that this is exactly what tends
to happen when I practice discursive meditations: They encourage
me to slow down and savor every aspect.

IGNATIAN MEDITATION

*Form a mental image of the scene and see in [the] imagination the road
from Nazareth to Bethlehem . . . consider its length and breadth, and
whether it is level or winding through valleys and other hills. Behold the
place of the cave of the Nativity, whether it is large or small, whether
high or low, and what it contains.*
　　　　　　　　　　　　　　—Ignatius Loyola, *Spiritual Exercises*

History and Background

Think back to a pivotal moment in your life or in the life of someone
close to you. In addition to the importance of the moment, almost
certainly you will remember certain sensory details: the way the sky
looked, the way the air felt, or the tone of someone's voice. While

these have nothing to do with real significance of the moment, we remember the sensory details as if they were part of the experience. That is part of being alive.

The persistence of sensory memories lies behind one of the most comprehensive and intentional systems of meditation ever developed. St. Ignatius Loyola's method is our most complicated approach to verbal meditation. Some find it impossibly complex; others find it irresistible. Anyone seriously interested in the art of keeping silence would do well to experiment with it at least for a while. For many people it is meditation at its best.

To understand Ignatius's system, it helps to know a little about his background. In the sixteenth century, an era of nationalist fervor and geographical expansion, Inigo Lopez de Recalde, a Spanish nobleman, served at the court of Ferdinand, the great explorer-king. Later, Recalde entered the military, where he made a name for himself as soldier. He might well have become known to history as a Spanish patriot, had he not been seriously wounded defending Pamplona against the rival French in 1521. His injury terminated his military career.

Ignatius, as he was known, spent his long recovery in prayer and study, reading the lives of the saints, medieval devotional books, and keeping the monastic hours, the monks' daily worship services. His life was transformed when he experienced a vision of himself as a soldier of Christ. All his loyalties shifted from crown to cross. Physically, Ignatius was unfit for service, but psychologically, he was fitter than ever. And this is the key to Ignatius's accomplishment.

That key is important, because it is very easy to misunderstand Ignatius's model. People outside the military think of soldiers as fighters. Those who have had military experience know better. A soldier's life is one of discipline, training, and preparation. Ignatius applied what he had learned from military discipline as he set about training his spirit.

He outlined a way of life centered on spiritual development—a kind of boot camp for the soul. At the center of his approach was meditation. He distilled centuries of contemplative experience into a clear-cut, comprehensive plan that included an annual, month-long retreat. Ignatius's plan was to involve every facet of the human personality—memory, reason, emotion, and imagination, will—in the work of meditation. In its original form, the Ignatian meditative exercise is complex and very difficult to practice; it requires spiritual guidance, even for those who are familiar with it. On the other hand, it often has been simplified, and many ordinary people have followed a modified version in the course of their daily lives. Condensed versions of the Ignatian exercises have proven to be extremely popular daily meditations.

Practicing

The meditation begins with a passage of Scripture, ideally an historical narrative from the Bible. Read the passage slowly and deliberately the night before you meditate. Ignatius calls this "remote preparation." Focus on learning the story well; note every detail. You should be able to paraphrase the story easily by the time you are done reading.

Proceed to the next stage the following day. Ignatius calls it the "composition of place." Recall the setting of the passage using all of your senses, one by one. What does the scene look like? What time of day is it, and what does the light look like? How does the air feel? Is it warm or cool, windy or still? What sort of surface are you standing or sitting on as you observe the scene? What do you smell there? What do the voices of the principal actors sound like? Are there any noises? Fix the scene in your mind as you enter it imaginatively, becoming a part of everything.

The meditation proper involves three stages, based on Aristotle and Thomas Aquinas's division of the human mind into three parts: reason, emotion, and will. Use reason first to consider the intellectual aspects of the passage: What does it mean? What theological or other intellectual problems does it raise? Here we can consider any of the kinds of literary or historical questions that modern biblical scholars tends to ask. What is the context of the passage? What is its genre? What was its historical setting?

Next, examine the emotional impact of the passage. How does it make you feel? How is God depicted: loving, just, implacable, merciful, or angry? Having placed ourselves in the scene, are we gratified? Uncomfortable? In this stage of the meditation, in contrast with the first, be as personal and as idiosyncratic as you please: You can dwell on private verbal associations that are meaningful to no one else. You can "read into" the texts anything at all, as long as these inferences arise from your emotions.

Finally, formulate a brief resolve based upon what you have read, thought, and felt. This resolution should be short, practical, and concrete—in other words, something you're likely to carry out. Ignatius considered this final stage to be crucial, because it connects the detached reason of the first step and the free-form emotional response of the second step to the external world, forcing us to find the moral impetus in any passage we have read.

Sample Meditation

As an example of Ignatius's method, consider Mark's account of Jesus' healing a leper, one of the earliest miracles.

A man suffering from a virulent skin disease came to him and pleaded on his knees saying, "If you are willing, you can cleanse me." Feeling sorry for him, Jesus stretched out his hand, touched him, and said to him, "I am willing. Be cleansed." And at once the skin disease left him and he was cleansed. And at once Jesus sternly sent him away and said to him, "Mind you tell no one anything, but go and show yourself to the priest, and make your offering for your cleansing prescribed by Moses as evidence to them." The man went away, but started freely proclaiming and telling the story everywhere, so that Jesus could no longer go openly into any town, but stayed outside in deserted places. Even so, people from all around kept coming to him. (Mark 1:40–45, NJV).

Read over this passage the evening before the meditation, and allow it to enter the deepest levels of your consciousness. Then practice composition of place: Imagine that you are witness to this scene. We are not told exactly where this event took place. All we know is that Jesus has been traveling all over Galilee, so you might imagine hilly country with a great lake not too far away. Picturing a great deal of detail is unnecessary and beside the point. Scripture itself is vague about physical details, though, so give your imagination free reign. You might imagine the bright sun and feel its warmth. You might add a breeze from the lake. If you imagine yourself sitting nearby, feel the rocky ground beneath you. If you wish, smell the moisture in the air, or inhale the smell of the rocks and sand.

Now picture Jesus: Don't worry about his appearance, simply picture him in any way that seems comfortable to you. The important thing is to bring him to life: Animate him with gestures; hear his voice. Too often when we "picture" Jesus, or any other biblical character, we do it quite literally, we see a still picture rather than a moving image. Here you should use your imagination to reproduce the effect of a living human being, one you can hear as well as see, one who speaks, breathes, and moves.

Hear the sound of his voice: In this case we are told he is "filled with pity." What does that sound like? Now see the sick man. We are told he has a skin disease, so you might include that in your image. You can see the man fall to his knees before Jesus or simply approach him boldly. The Gospel is characteristically reticent about these details, so you are free to imagine him in any posture, with any gesture, and any kind of voice you wish.

The classic procedure is to go through the senses one by one: First ask, What do I see? Then, What do I hear? and so on. I have found it just as productive to imagine the parts of the scene, one by one, as I have suggested here. Use whichever method works best for you. The point is to explore freely until you have entered the biblical scene. With a little practice, it becomes quite easy.

Next, shift gears and engage your reasoning powers. Open to the Bible passage and note where it appears, in this case, very early in

the Gospel. We have been told that Jesus healed many others earlier, but this is the first story where the details of the healing are
shown. What does that mean? How does Jesus perform the miracle? What words are exchanged? What does it mean for the man to
ask Jesus whether he wants to heal him or not, rather than Jesus
asking the victim whether he wants to be healed? Is it significant
that Jesus gives instructions that comply with the Law of Moses?
What do you make of Jesus asking the man to tell no one about it?
And why does the man do the exact opposite?

Now skim through the Gospel and briefly notice other healing
stories. How is this one different? How is it typical? Second, skip to
the other Gospels and see whether there are any patterns to healing
stories, and whether this one is typical, or anomalous. Third, com-
pare this version of the story with versions in any of the other
Gospels, if you can (a Bible with good footnotes or marginal references will be helpful here). How does Mark's version differ from
the others?

These are the kinds of questions scholars ask about the text, and
they don't have all the answers. Don't worry whether your answers
are right or wrong—there's no such thing. Simply wrestle with the
questions for a few moments to the best of your ability. In this story
you are trying to engage the rational side of your mind. You are trying to use your head. Then, ask yourself what it all seems to add up
to. What does it mean for Jesus to accomplish his first detailed
healing miracle in this manner? Why is his volition a key element
in the story? What does Jesus' "pity" have to do with it? What kind
of man, and what kind of God, is involved here?

Ignatian meditation may prove difficult at first. Don't be concerned about that; it gets easier as you go along and develop the
necessary mental habits. Soon it will feel like second nature. To
excel at any skill you need practice.

Next, proceed to explore the passage from an emotional perspective. How do you feel about this story? How does it make you feel
about Jesus? About God? About any other characters? The composition of place you have already practiced may come in handy here. It
can help you to discover your genuine feeling for a biblical passage,

rather than the conventional feelings most of us think we are supposed to have. For example, in a group meditation on the text we have been using, several people were startled to discover that their first real emotional response was fear. They thought they were supposed to feel respect and love for Jesus, or some such pious feeling, but when they felt free to imagine themselves in the scene, responding as eyewitnesses, they realized that they would be frightened if they saw such a thing happen.

The final step springs from the second one. Describe what the passage impels you to do. Most people find it relatively easy to formulate this resolution, perhaps because the steps we take in Ignatian meditation are exactly like the steps we take in real life. We experience something vividly with our senses, we think about it very deliberately, and we get in touch with our feelings as we respond to what we've witnessed.

The key here is to keep the resolution small. Having engaged the feelings and the intellect so strongly, having so effectively entered the scene and identified with the characters, many people tend to overextend themselves in the act of resolution. They tend to make their resolution either too big or too abstract. Consider, for example, an act of the will based on the beatitudes. You've entered the scene and imagined yourself there on the mount, listening to Jesus' sermon. You have thought it through, and examined your feelings. You have responded powerfully with your thoughts and feelings. You are especially drawn to the teaching "blessed are the peacemakers," and you determine to do something about peace. So you decide to canvass your community and organize a letter-writing campaign to your congressman in hopes of enacting some peace-keeping legislation. Or, you determine to "work for world peace." Obviously, either one is a worthy resolve, but neither one is a good conclusion for Ignatian meditation. The first is too big: It cannot be accomplished in a day, or even in a week. The second sounds very good, but is practically meaningless; it's too abstract to translate into direct action. And taking action is exactly what the third and final step of Ignatian meditation is all about.

A good Ignatian resolution can be carried out by the end of the day. A better response to the text, "Blessed are the peacemakers," might be a single act, such as a telephone call to your legislator. That can be accomplished by nightfall.

In order to have a high likelihood of success, your resolution should not require heroism, discomfort, or expense. All a resolution should involve is will, not courage, physical fitness, or risk. It should be something you *can do*, without a doubt, as long as you are willing. It should not require any great expenditure on your part. Heroism is admirable and sometimes necessary, but no one can exhibit it on a daily basis. Keep your Ignatian resolution clear, simple, and do-able.

CHAPTER FIVE

Kinetic Meditations

I have always been intrigued with the fact that the English words *holy*, *whole*, and *health* all derive from the Indo-European root *hl*. I believe languages retain deep wisdom, that etymological facts are never merely coincidences. Our language here reflects a real connection between health and faith—between body and soul.

Our final methods for keeping silence are based on that connection. More than any other way of meditating, and in complete contrast to mental prayer, these *walking meditations* or *kinetic* methods involve the body. In sitting meditations, posture is important, but primarily as a means of freeing the soul; kinetic meditations use the body to express the soul. The rhythm of physical movement replaces the rhythm of breath, vision, or thought.

Kinetic meditation is like dance. Unlike that art form, however, kinetic meditations require no special aptitude or training. Anyone who is ambulatory can do them. In fact, as we shall see, the physically gifted person has no real advantage. So while the physically active person may find them congenial, so might the sedentary person who feels the need for something a little different in his or her meditative life. I have seen people who are ordinarily very quiet and physically inexpressive find kinetic meditations to be downright liberating. Almost anyone who tries them finds them a powerful and surprising way of entering stillness.

WALKING MEDITATION

I will walk in the presence of the Lord.
—Psalm 116:8, BCP

History and Background

Have you ever watched a big cat pacing? Maybe you've seen one at the zoo, or watched them on a television program. Lions, panthers, and tigers pace, not only in the confines of the old-fashioned and cruel zoo cages, but in the wide-open spaces as well. So if you can, take a trip to the local zoo or wild animal park. If you can't do that, just imagine one of the big cats as you read.

First, take in the fluidity of the cat. She really does seem to flow. Note how powerful she is as well. Imagine how it would feel if there were no barriers between you and the cat. Now notice the control she exhibits. You may be surprised to discover that she takes the same number of steps in one direction as she does in the other. Note her velocity: How many steps does she take per second, or how many seconds per step? Actually time her next time you see a big cat in person: Remember that pace.

Then, look at the placement of her feet. One foot is perfectly aligned behind the other, front-to-front, back-to-back. Take away the ground in your imagination: She could be tightrope walking, so perfectly does she place her feet. Contemplate her on that rope for a moment. Feel how she carries her great, four-hundred-pound body, which is centered with a lightness and grace our much smaller species rarely exhibits. Watch her head, and the ridge on the top of her back. Her body doesn't bob up and down, or wag from side to side.

If you haven't already imagined how it feels to be the pacing cat, try being her now. Feel the cat with your body, just as you would sway along to the feel of music. Get into her skin and try to sense what it feels like to walk that way.

If you like to draw, make a sketch of the cat. If not, draw a sketch in the air with your finger; artists call this "blind drawing." Don't look at your sketching hand, only at the outlines of the animal. And try to remember not only what you see, but also what you feel as you draw.

Now notice one final aspect of the cat's action: her breathing. Great cats carry very little surface fat, so you can see the ribcage and the muscles all along her flanks, which makes it easy to follow her breath. Fix on that for a few moments. Count her breaths from one to fifty. You may find yourself coordinating your own breath with hers. Watch how the lion's stride is coordinated with her own breath as well.

What you have just experienced is in itself a meditation, and a very exquisite one. Such an imaginative and empathetic encounter with another living creature is encouraged in the yogic tradition, and in some schools of Buddhism. They commend this practice, in part, because it is deeply centering, but it is also an important way to experience our kinship with other beings. It can even turn a visit to a zoo or other animal shelter into a rewarding meditative affair.

But that's not why I introduced this meditation here. It's not the lion I want you to experience, it's her walk. She is a wonderful teacher of the walking meditation, which is a classic way to quiet the mind.

Practicing

In Christian tradition, walking has always been linked to deep communion with God. Two Scriptural sources lie behind this association. First, Genesis 3.8 mentions God walking in the garden of Eden "in the cool of the evening." Patristic writers extended this notion to the idea that Adam and God often walked together before the Fall. So walking became a reminder not only of our original condition, but also of the means to recover a portion of it. Second, "walking" is one of the most frequently mentioned verbs in the Book of Psalms, the Scriptural sourcebook for the life of prayer. "I will walk in the presence of the Lord," as our epigram from Psalm 116 says, and such verses reinforce the idea that walking, when practiced with mindfulness, is a sacred act.

But awareness is the key. It's what separates prayerful walking from ordinary locomotion, just as mindful breathing differs from ordinary oxidation. For your walking meditation, choose a space with at least twelve feet of room to walk. A shorter space will work if necessary, but a longer one is easiest. The space can be inside or outside, though generally something inside provides more privacy. Remove your shoes, and socks, if possible. Practicing a walking meditation with shoes is like trying to thread a needle with mittens: possible, but needlessly difficult. You'll want to be able to feel the ground beneath your feet in this meditation.

First, if you were able to watch a great cat, copy her. Emulate her walk, and, as in the empathetic meditation we did, try to feel her feelings. Become the cat. If you could not observe an actual cat, do this imaginatively. Walk twelve feet, turn, and walk back.

Now try to do it systematically. Instead of simply walking along mindlessly, walk deliberately and with full mindfulness, or awareness. Imagine a straight line on the ground, and put one foot in front of the other as the cat did. Count your steps, if that helps. If counting confuses you, just forget it.

Sometimes people find this surprisingly difficult. It is another example of our paradox of simplicity and ease: What is simple is not necessarily easy. We are so used to using our feet automatically, it becomes difficult for us to use them deliberately. Practice this exercise until you can do it with awareness, and as easily as what you normally do mindlessly. This alone may take ten minutes of silence.

Whenever this way of walking becomes natural, add this: Stop for a moment at each step, just as brides do when they are walking down the aisle. Feel and enjoy the subtle rhythm this creates. When stopping with each step becomes easy, try to coordinate your steps with your breath. I find a simple inhale-step, exhale-step works for me, but discover your own rhythm here. You are doing what world-champion runners do, who depend on proper oxygenation. They know exactly how many strides they take per inhalation. You're doing the same thing in slow motion.

Coordinating your steps and breaths may take practice. As you experiment with coordinating your walking and breathing, explore the rhythm and the sensations you feel. Notice your breathing, and hear it, just as you did in the seated breathing practice. Hear that soft teakettle sound at the back of the throat. Let that be your silent sound, the one that dispels all other noise from your environment, from your life, for these ten protected minutes. Picture your breath as a liquid, entering through your head and moving deep into your being. Imagine it pouring in all the way down to your pelvic region, which you are using to breathe deeply. This will help deepen the silence, just as it did in seated meditations.

Experience the way various moods and circumstances affect your meditative work. If you are worried and tense, it may be more difficult to get your walking and breath coordinated, or you may find it easier to coordinate the two. Your ten-minute walking meditation may be a stress reliever that relaxes your breath. Experience and explore.

When you have coordinated your steps and your breath starts to feel natural, begin to notice the various parts of your body as you walk. Feel the soles of your feet—noticing what portions of your feet actually touch the floor. (Some practitioners find it helpful to use another image here. Imagine you have the feet of an ape, capable of grasping and articulation.) Picture your feet gripping the surface. Do you walk from heel to toe? Flatfooted? Do you tend to roll your foot from inside out, or from outside in? Note the flexing of your ankle, the work of your arch, and the movement of your toes. All these things happen whenever you walk; all you are doing here is practicing awareness.

Gradually, move your awareness up from your feet. Notice the feeling in your Achilles tendon, the flexing of your calf. How many times in the course of the day do you ask your calf to flex? Feel the very taut muscle sheaf on the front of your lower leg as it subtly lifts the toes each time you take a step. Many mystics have noticed the miracles in such minuscule natural creations as a blade of grass or a pebble; you are doing exactly that with your lower body.

Don't think too much about what you are doing. Simply feel the sensations: the alternating tension and relaxation, pressure and release. Feel the bending and straightening of your knees, the flexion and extension of your thighs, the swing and the thrust of your gluteal muscles, your lower back, and abdomen.

As you continue this practice, return to an awareness of your breath from time to time. If you lose your coordination, return to the previous movement until you recover it. After a while, it becomes automatic. As you become more adept, you may notice that your rhythm changes as the ratio of breath to step changes. Allow this to happen, but allow it to happen mindfully. And visualize the great cat: Remember her vividly expanding ribcage.

Now move your attention to your upper body. What are your arms doing? How do they coordinate with your feet? Does your right arm swing forward as your right leg retracts? Do your shoulders sway from side to side, or are they straightforward? Are your fists clenched, or your hands open? Most people clench their fists hard when they want to run as fast as possible, but some of the best sprinters leave their hands open. Try various things with your hands. Discover what feels best.

Note your spine, and the position of your head. Are you looking at your feet? After practicing a while, try lifting your eyes toward the horizon or a spot on a wall. Your balance will eventually improve if you do this: Looking at your feet impairs graceful walking. Think of your focal point—the horizon or the spot on the wall—as the point toward which your whole person is moving. That is what the cat does: She never looks down, unless something really interesting crosses her path.

Although your feet are in motion, try to keep your head and shoulders within the same vertical plane. Imagine a ceiling one-half inch above your head, and try to avoid bobbing up and down. Your feet rise and fall, but your head moves through space in a single straight line. Imagine that, practice and feel it.

Are you frowning? Scowling? Is your face knit in concentration? Try to replace that expression with a slight smile. Try to relax the planes of your face. Are you squinting? Try to open your eyes comfortably wide. Relax your neck and forehead.

Treat all these suggestions lightly. They are suggestions rather than a set of instructions you must follow in sequence. If at any point you find yourself confused or frustrated by my suggestions, ignore them. Simply practice the act of walking mindfully, one step in front of the other, through your fixed distance, to and fro.

At some point in your experiment with walking meditation, study your reactions to your 180-degree turn at either end of the path. We all turn naturally every day, but rarely notice what actually happens. Notice which foot pivots. Do you pivot on the heel, or the ball of the foot, or at the center? Do you pivot on one foot, or both feet? Do you turn the same way every time, or do you find yourself improvising throughout your meditation? What does your way of turning say about how you feel? Do you swing your body around in a sort of pirouette, or step briskly into the new direction? What happens to your arms and hands? Does your head duck, or circle ahead or behind the rest of the body? Are you turning the way our friend the great cat turns? Do you shut your eyes as you spin? Again, these are just suggestions about things to notice, not questions you have to answer.

Gradually is an important word in this kind of meditation: It comes from the Latin word for *step*. If you enjoy this meditation, you will eventually take thousands of steps along your simple path: literal steps. Every step can be a progression in silence. There is never a need to hurry because you are learning and making progress no matter what happens. If one day you feel distracted throughout, just do the best you can for ten minutes. Let whatever is distracting you join you for the walk that day. It may help, and it can't hurt.

CLOISTER WALKING

One shall not go about the cloister like the impious, in circles along paths of vanity and curiosity, but like the angels he shall climb Jacob's ladder.
                                        —*De disciplina claustri,* 12th century

The word *cloister* originally came from the word *claustrum,* which meant simply "the bar that secures a door." The modern dead bolt is a type of claustrum. Eventually, however, cloisters came to refer to monasteries, buildings where monks lived apart from the rest of the world. The word also refers to the long open walkways along the monastery's outside walls. The roofs to these porch-like galleries are held up by pillars connected by arches, which frame a central garden space. These cloisters are a feature of the vast majority of Western medieval monasteries. Cloisters are situated immediately adjacent to the chapel or main church. A door or gateway provides instant access between cloister and chapel. Chapel and cloister together constituted the heart of the monastery: the right and left ventricles of that heart. You carried your chapel experience with you into the cloister, and your cloister experience with you into the chapel, hour after hour, day after day.

Besides being beautiful, the cloister is functional. It provides a soothing setting for solitary prayer and meditation. The architecture itself enhances spiritual practices. Today, most people understandably think of meditating "in a church," but that's not the way monastic buildings work. Monks pray together in church, but they often meditate or say their private prayers in the semi-outdoor cloisters.

While some monks sit in the spaces provided by the arcade, many of them walk around the cloister while praying or meditating. There are spots to practice the sitting meditation on the psalms or lessons they just heard in church. The long open cloister is the perfect place to practice kinetic meditation. As the epigraph for this section suggests, they are to be making heavenly progress; though they literally walk in circles, spiritually they are climbing.

Practicing

If you have the opportunity to visit a monastery or any other setting that happens to have a cloistered walkway, you can experience this for yourself. Simply take a psalm, or a portion of a psalm, and repeat it, while walking. By "take," I mean literally: Open a Bible or prayer book, or make a copy in your own hand (better still, in fact). Do not try to memorize it, but if that happens, as it sometimes will, fine; then, as we saw when we experimented with memorization, you "own" the psalm at a deeper level. Do not simply "think" it, however. Murmur the words softly. If you like, coordinate your psalm recitation with the architectural elements of the arcade. Speak one verse, or half a verse as you pass each arch, depending on your tempo and on the length of the arches. Just as you coordinated step and breath in the simple walking meditation, now you coordinate step and psalm.

The coordination of your step and speaking the psalm is easy—this is not a coincidence. The medieval cloister was designed with walking meditation in mind. We even know of some cloisters that were built to contain exactly as many units as there are verses in the processional psalm for their patron's feast day. That way, on each patron's festival, the procession would begin and end at exactly the same spot. One immediate effect of this practice is to make all walking more meditative. Just as silence makes us more deliberate when we use words, so deliberate walking has this carryover effect in our everyday locomotion. We come to associate walking with psalms, so that whenever we walk, we take the psalm along without thinking.

It is not necessary to visit a monastery to practice this kind of meditation; you can practice it anywhere. And you can use tiles in a floor, panels along a wall, cracks in a sidewalk, or columns in a long room to imitate the cloisterlike effect. Just coordinate your recitation of the psalm with whatever floor or wall pattern you have available.

To demonstrate the difference between the sitting and the walking versions of this meditation, try sitting for five minutes and simply think about some psalm verse. Don't worry about paying attention to your breath or heartbeat. Don't repeat the psalm silently or aloud. Forget about every practice we've learned so far. Just think about the psalm verse. Then, for five minutes, walk the psalm, using any aspect of mindfulness you like. What is the difference?

When we simply sit and think it over, it is practically impossible *not to* consider the meaning of a psalm, its use, its theology, and so forth. When we walk and repeat it rhythmically, just the opposite happens. It's almost impossible *to* think about the psalm theologically or intellectually. The thoughts that come when we ruminate on the psalm in walking meditation are almost inevitably of a different order entirely from the rational thoughts we entertain when we sit and think. To some, reciting the psalm while walking may still seem strange. In fact, it is quite congruent with the original practice of psalmody, according to most scholars. Many of the psalms, it is generally agreed, were intended originally for just such kinetic use. A number were written to accompany a coronation procession: A new king entered his capital with his retinue, and the crowd chanted the psalm, step by step in time with the procession.

THE LABYRINTH

History and Background

The labyrinth—a maze for meditative walking—has enjoyed increased popularity in recent years. These visual relics from the Middle Ages are actually a mystery to us. They weren't mentioned in any documents or letters from monastic communities, so we can only guess at how they were used originally. The best known, the labyrinth at Chartres Cathedral in France, measures forty-two feet in diameter, with paths that are uniformly about one foot wide. Many people assume it was used for meditative walking, or perhaps crawling during the penitential season of Lent.

Just as a side note, the name *labyrinth* is actually a misnomer. Real labyrinths were terrible places. King Minos made the artisan Daedalus design a labyrinth, where he kept the Minotaur, the half-human, half-bovine monster. Theseus, the hero, managed to escape from the labyrinth by means of a divine ruse. *Labyrinth* is the Greek word for a convoluted, baffling structure, full of blind passages and false starts—in other words, a maze. But for whatever reason, the term has been applied to the large floor designs found embedded in the floors of several early Gothic and late Romanesque cathedrals. Since we have no other word for the labyrinth, we continue to use that word.

Whatever its original name, I believe it was originally intended to help its users achieve a meditative state wordlessly, and then to move on to contemplation. The churches and cathedrals where labyrinths were situated provided rich material for contemplation: The stained glass and stone images depicted all the major Bible stories, and provided a complete course in picture and symbol of theology, ethics, the sacraments, and prayer. Whatever its original purpose, those who have experimented with the great floor pattern today all seem to agree that it is almost uncanny in its capacity for teaching the art of meditation.

Practicing

If you are fortunate enough to have access to a labyrinth, or able to construct one for yourself, you can test this claim. Enter the patterned path anywhere along the periphery, and follow it until you reach the center. Everything we have said about walking meditation applies here. Walk slowly and deliberately, one foot in front of the other, posture straight but relaxed. Be aware of how you place your foot; coordinate your stride with your breath, lower your gaze slightly, but hold your head erect; focus your mind on the simple act of walking. Those who have practiced kinetic meditation, or any other form, will take to the patterned path naturally. But even the person unused to meditation in any form will discover most of these precepts naturally as he or she goes along.

There is no predetermined thing you should meditate on as you walk the maze. You may wish to enter the path with a specific intention, need, or hope in mind, or you may walk the labyrinth with a clear and quiet mind. As with any journey, pay attention to your thoughts, prayers, or anything else that comes to mind as you work your way to the center. It is not unusual to "hear" a message or thought that is important for your life. Unless you have your own private labyrinth, there may be other people walking the path at the same time. Be aware of them, without needing to pay any attention to what they are doing. If you come near to someone else, simply make way and continue along your path.

At the center of the labyrinth is a circle where you can stand or sit for as long as you like. Linger there to contemplate the journey so far. When you have finished your meditation, walk the path back to the beginning in a slow, meditative, and deliberate fashion. When you leave the labyrinth you may want to take some additional time to rest and contemplate whatever came to you while walking. If at all possible, it is best to make a gentle transition from the quiet journey of the labyrinth to your daily activities.

The experience of the labyrinth tends to be remarkably similar for all that try it, including those with no particular theological belief. It also tends to happen much the same way no matter how often we practice it.

Both beginners and those with experience in walking the labyrinth experience self-consciousness. This self-consciousness manifests itself in two ways. First, we may feel abnormally aware of our place in the surroundings. This is what we normally mean by self-consciousness, and anyone who begins to walk a labyrinth experiences it. But unlike ordinary self-consciousness, which is felt most strongly or even exclusively when others are present, this self-consciousness does not seem to depend on our sense of other people. It is equally strong when we walk the labyrinth in total solitude. We may feel awkward and strange, and uncomfortably aware of our bodies and minds.

As we place one foot in front of the other, however, this feeling quickly subsides. We progress just slightly inward on the gentle spiraling path, and self-consciousness gives way to a sense of strength, of "rightness," as our minds, bodies, and hearts work on the simple

challenge of staying on the path.But then a second level of awareness manifests itself. We know that this is supposed to be a form of
meditation, and that it is supposed to have some kind of Christian
content. We know that we are supposed to get something out of
this, that somehow this meditation should make us better people or
better Christians—"better" in whatever way, and we start to see the
practice as empty and futile. We are not repeating Bible verses, or
saying prayers, or looking at Christian signs or at images of Scriptural stories. This is a second, deeper level of self-consciousness,
more powerful than the first.

The familiar critical voice now takes advantage of this. You
"should" be doing something more productive with your limited
time, it tells you. If you want to be religious, you should be praying.
Or at least studying Scripture, or reading one of the spiritual classics. Better still, you could be alleviating human misery by working
for some charitable service. You should be in the soup kitchen, not
here. At least you could be practicing a form meditation that has
some real Christian content, if you must spend your valuable time
in this way. You could at least be saying the Jesus Prayer. All you are
doing is walking a silly diagram.

It is helpful to acknowledge this voice, and then dismiss it for
now. You can do those other things the voice suggests at another
time, but for now, just tell the voice that right now you are walking
the labyrinth. Simply keep going, keep making progress, even as the
voice persists.

As you move further in, toward the center of the labyrinth, this
second level of self-consciousness also begins to melt away, and the
voice ceases. What replaces it is not a sense of victory, but one of
positive emptiness. Self-consciousness is a very unpleasant feeling;
it involves a sense of restriction, as though the world is too "tight"
for us. Walking the narrow, convoluted path of the labyrinth paradoxically first creates, then dissolves, this feeling, and the sense of
release is almost inevitable, no matter how often we practice it.

The second self-critical voice, which objects to what we might
call the "nondenominational" nature of the labyrinth—its lack of

overt Christian content—no longer seems to make any sense. For along with the sense of emptiness, we soon sense a welcome divine presence. Not in any shattering sense, not in the sense of a sudden rapture or conversion. In fact, quite the opposite. But very definitely, we sense God's presence—or, at least, that we are in the presence of God.

As we continue, it can become clear why this presence feels quietly assuring rather than extraordinary. We realize that this is the normal condition: God is always present. We know this philosophically—intellectually—but most of the time we do not sense it or feel it. The labyrinth, because it not only centers us but forces us to confront, then get rid of, our self-consciousness, allows this perception. Others may express this feeling differently, but in every case this comforting, gentle presence is what people experience as they approach the center of the path. I suspect this is the reason many become such loyal devotees of the labyrinth.

THE WAY OF THE CROSS

Mercifully grant that we, walking in the way of the cross,
may find it none other than the way of life and peace.
—Collect at the First Station

History and Background

In the fourth century, Constantine made Christianity legal and it became the official religion of the Roman Empire. Before that time, Christians had been persecuted, but his complete reversal of fortune led to all sorts of opportunities for Christians and their churches. Individual Christians were also free now to travel openly. The Holy Land now became a popular destination for pilgrimage, as Christians from across the Empire arrived there to revisit the sacred Biblical and historical sites, to stand on sacred ground. The Emperor's mother, Helena, supposedly recovered the cross Christ died on during one of her journeys, even as the emperor banned crucifixion as a legal punishment.

The most popular time to visit Jerusalem was, of course, during Holy Week, and so began a tradition that continues to this day. Fortunately, a Spanish nun, Egeria (or "Etheira") left a journal in which she records her various pilgrimages, including just such a Holy Week sojourn in the ancient capital. It is invaluable for the light it sheds on monastic practices at that point in time, on liturgy as it was developing during this rich and creative period, and on the contemporary understanding of Scripture. But above all, it is priceless for its detailed sketch of Holy Week devotions.

These devotions involved a full three-day meditation on the last days of Jesus, beginning at night on Holy Thursday. The worshipers would gather at the supposed site of the Lord's Supper. Then, singing anthems, they would process to the Garden of Gethsemane. Then, late at night, to the high priest's palace, and early in the morning, to Pilate's *praetorium*. From there, they greeted the dawn by walking the Via Dolorosa through the winding streets of old Jerusalem, stopping along the way at the spots where Jesus was supposed to have stumbled; finally they would halt outside the city at Golgotha. After three hours, they concluded with a procession to the supposed site of the tomb.

This experience, as Egeria tells us, was profoundly moving, and it was one of the primary reasons Jerusalem continued to attract pilgrims throughout the Middle Ages and down to the present day. But a pilgrimage to the Holy Land was either dangerous or expensive, or both. For many people, it was out of the question. Besides, even for the hardy and for the well-to-do, it had to be a rare or once-in-a-lifetime event. Nobody could, or can, afford to make the pilgrimage every year.

But Holy Week comes every year. And so inventive Christians soon realized that they did not have to travel to the Holy Land to share this devotional experience. A "virtual" Via Dolorosa could be improvised anywhere. By the fifth century, stylized reminders of the road to Calvary began to appear throughout Europe. Within church buildings or outside, these consisted of images of the Gospel events: Jesus in the garden, Jesus before the High Priests, and so on.

The service was also shortened. Just as few people could afford to visit the Holy Land, few could devote the entire four days from Holy Thursday to Easter Sunday to their devotions. The shorter version that resulted focused on the events of Good Friday mentioned in the four gospels—the events on the way to the cross.

The service that eventually resulted was the Way (or Stations) of the Cross: a walking meditation based on the crucial events of Good Friday. In its most ancient form, the Way of the Cross was simply a rectangular or elliptical path with fourteen stations, meaning "places where you stand," marked by a cross. At each of these stations, prayers were said, and a recounting of the event was read. Quite early in the tradition, it seems, the following fourteen events became standard: Jesus' trial (the one Thursday event), Jesus taking up the cross, Jesus falling, Jesus encountering Mary his mother, Simon of Cyrene relieving Jesus of the cross, Veronica wiping Jesus' face, Jesus falling again, the women of Jerusalem and Jesus' prophecy over them, Jesus' third fall, Jesus stripped of his garments, the soldiers nailing Jesus to the cross, Jesus' death, Jesus in the arms of his mother, and Jesus laid in the tomb.

Eventually, the prayers at each station became more or less fixed; Roman Catholic and Episcopal texts for the Way of the Cross are nearly identical for this reason. Even more impressively, in many church buildings, depictions of the events came to be included along with the simple crosses, and these depictions could become quite elaborate, even works of art in their own right. Finally, the hymn *Stabat Mater* came increasingly to be used as a processional hymn for those moving from station to station.

Practicing

These various elaborations of the original concept, explained above, are definitely helpful when "doing the Stations" as a group. The hymn, the visual depictions, and the fixed prayer forms help unify the experience for all. But they are less necessary to us when we are praying the Way of the Cross on our own. All we really need to follow the stations is the list above and a few simple crosses—and even these are not strictly necessary. The Way of the Cross can be practiced anywhere where movement is allowed, just like any walking meditation.

Many convents, monasteries, and churches, particularly Roman Catholic ones, have the Stations of the Cross set up permanently in their buildings or on their grounds, and these are generally available to the public. But if you want to set up your own permanent or temporary stations, use fourteen crosses or other religious objects and set them up with some space between them—at least ten feet or more. Before you begin, take a few moments to quiet and center yourself. Then walk to the first station, read the story associated with that particular station, and then take a few moments to contemplate that part of the gospel story. Then walk to the next station, and so on until you complete all fourteen of them.

What is indispensable when practicing the Way of the Cross is precisely the kind of mindful walking that we have described. An ordinary mindless amble from place to place will not work here. The movement must be slow, deliberate, and conscious.

THE BOOK OF THE POOR

I bless you, Father, Lord of heaven and of earth, for hiding these things from the learned and clever and revealing them to little children.
—Matthew 11:25, NJB

History and Background

The Gothic church building was known as the *liber pauporum,* the "poor people's book," because the walls, windows, and practically any other visible space were adorned with Bible stories and other images that taught important lessons. The illiterate masses, who before Gutenberg could not have bought a book even if they had learned to read, "read" their church walls to learn the faith.

Churches before the Gothic period (which began with the work of Abbot Suger in the 12th century) were designed solely for communal worship, rather than for private prayer and devotion. Gothic churches, on the other hand, were designed not only with the liturgy in mind, but also for private use. Even today, their windows and other artwork continue to be splendid catalysts for private meditation.

Practicing

Before meditating on the art in a church you'll need to know a little about how the church depicts stories in its windows and art. In the windows, and in statuary inside and outside the building, you find events from the life of Christ, figures and stories from the Old Testament, the lives of the saints, or abstractions (such as faith, hope, and love) depicted in Christian symbols. Before meditating on any particular point, most find it helpful to sort all this out, to understand how this Bible in glass and stone has been organized.

The earliest Gothic church buildings were planned according to a very simple scheme. Abbot Suger of the Royal Abbey of St. Denis, the first completely Gothic building, was deeply influenced by the thought of an anonymous sixth-century mystic who assumed the name of the "Dionysius" Paul converted in the Book of Acts. This "Dionysius" teaches that light is our most immediately accessible symbol of heaven: God's first creation was light, and so light is literally heaven on earth.

Suger incorporated light into his scheme for decorating church surfaces. In addition to the outside, which for several centuries had been adorned with more and more statues depicting Bible stories and Christian truths, Suger now had at his disposal vast stained glass surfaces in the windows, thanks to the architectural technology of the 12th century. He devised a rough scheme: Exterior surfaces would focus on Old Testament figures, so statues of kings and prophets often adorn the outside. Inside, stained or painted glass would present, at the lower levels, New Testament scenes, and in the higher ranges, scenes depicting the life of heaven or eternal realities, such as abstract truths or Christian symbols. For example, you may find a sculpted figure of Eve in a scene from Genesis near the entrance, a depiction of the Annunciation in a lower register window, and the figure of Mary as Queen of Heaven in the Rose window dominating the western facade.

This plan, however, was only an organizing principle, never a rigid rule. You will also find Annunciations in stone on the outside, and Old Testament scenes in the windows, and depictions of the Last Judgment around the entranceways—a heritage from the earlier Romanesque artists, who liked to present visions from the book of Revelation where they could confront the worshipper entering the church. Every Gothic building expresses its personality through its variations of Suger's simple three-part scheme.

Some of the larger cathedrals provide handbooks that offer suggestions about these matters, as well as interesting background information. But it is really up to the viewer to discover for him- or herself the logic and the patterning. A Gothic church, especially a cathedral, was designed to be a vast encyclopedia of Christian truth. Like the great theological encyclopedias, the Summas, which were written during the same era, the building was intended to be all-inclusive. Explore it the way you would explore a vast and rich reference work—let your instincts and interests be your best guide.

The same principle applies to individual windows. There is no single rule of organization; every window in a given church follows its own logic. Try reading it from bottom to top, rather than from top to bottom; try reading right to left rather than left to right. Our spatial conventions—left to right and top to bottom—were developed much later.

All this information is to prepare you for the meditation, just as we went over the history of icons before the icon meditation. When confronted with the massive brilliance of a Gothic church, most people want some sense of the overall scheme. Try to discover that scheme for yourself; it was meant to be discovered that way. This may take some time and more than one visit; in larger churches, binoculars may be helpful. In the great medieval cathedrals, some items were placed very high up; in that pretelescopic era, these objects were not meant for human, but for angelic, viewing.

Once you have acquired some sense of the overall pattern, begin to narrow your focus. Start by walking around the space once or twice, pausing briefly at each image, just as you would when praying the Stations of the Cross. Before the image, pray a short prayer asking for God's blessing through this medium; then simply look and enjoy. That's all you want to do for your first session.

Then, when you feel ready, pick an image to focus on. This image can be anything: as I have suggested, the classic Gothic cathedrals tried to express the whole of reality, and their modern neo-Gothic American counterparts often mimic them. I recommend starting with either a person, a biblical scene, or a symbol: for example, an image of a saint or a symbol of one of the sacraments. You already have some experience with meditating with these kinds of images. Your experience will help now, in the more visually spectacular realm of the Gothic church.

Sit near the image at a time when you can view it undisturbed for fifteen minutes, and simply enjoy looking at it. Then, proceed as we did with the icon. Deal with the aesthetic issues if you need or want to. Any other aspect that comes to mind can also be addressed and acknowledged: How much did this window cost? When was this sculpture executed? What style is it? And so forth.

Finally, enter the image meditatively. You can use the same techniques we used with icons here; stained glass is the Western equivalent of the classic Eastern mosaic or icon. Place yourself in the presence of the person depicted in the window, just as we did with the icons. Feel the beauty and the power suggested and conveyed there.

Alternatively, the Ignatian approach, with its methodical use of the imagination, works very well in such a setting, particularly if the images portray biblical stories. An image from the New Testament, such as Jesus' feeding of the multitudes, can provide an extremely powerful meditation. Try engaging your senses: feel the breeze, smell the grass on the hillside, and so forth, and then use the three-part response of reason, emotion, and will.

At your next session, move to the image adjacent to the one you just explored. Gradually, over a period of days or weeks, move around the entire church, approaching each image using the same meditative technique. This technique can be a most comprehensive and satisfying way of reading the *liber pauporum* (the book of the poor), and it leaves you feeling that you truly understand the church's space. It is a good way either to become spiritually acquainted with a new church, or to deepen your spiritual sense of an old familiar one.

CHAPTER SIX

Extending the Silence

Any trial whatsoever that comes to you may be conquered by silence.
—Abbot Pastor

If you're still reading, the chances are that silence appeals to you. By now you have probably made silence a part of your routine, or at least you are seriously thinking about doing so. But if you find yourself wanting to deepen the place of silence in your life, here are some additional suggestions.

Take advantage of occasions when you are passively thrown into silence.

Most of us hate "wasted" time during the day, times when we can't do anything. We have to wait in a line somewhere, or we get stuck in traffic. Use these moments as opportunities to practice silence. Ruminate on the morning's lessons, practice your breath awareness, or chant a psalm.

Use your practice of silence to enrich your experience of corporate worship.

Many of our worship services provide excellent opportunities to practice silence, and corporate worship is always enhanced by those who understand the value of silence. Sunday morning services that include the Eucharist allow for periods of silence. Some congregations observe a few moments of silence after the Bible readings, which give you time to contemplate them. There are also a variety of occasional services that include ample silent time. Compline, the last of the evening services before bedtime, is a prelude to many hours of silence. In monasteries, the time after Compline, and before the first morning service, is called the Grand or Great Silence, something you may be able to observe on your own. Holy Week—the week between Palm Sunday and Easter, also includes a variety of services, such as Tenebrae, the Maundy Thursday watch, Good Friday services, and the Easter Vigil, all of which provide periods for silent contemplation.

Supplement your daily silence with a longer weekly silence.

We don't often observe the Sabbath in today's culture, but most of us need the rest and restoration Sabbath provides. Take a mini-Sabbath each week by observing silence for an extended period of time. I find that keeping a silent morning every week enhances my focus and refreshes me. It also makes my daily silence deeper and more effective, and heightens my awareness of the value and power of words.

Take a silent retreat every year.

Unlike the daily meditations that can be done in your home or in places you frequent daily, an annual silent retreat should be done someplace away from your daily environment. There are retreat possibilities almost anywhere—in urban as well as rural settings. Silent retreats can last from two days to thirty days, and most retreat centers can help you set one up and assist you during the retreat.

Find places to practice silence in your daily life.

Seek out silent places you can access when you want to have some intentional silence. These might be churches, parks, or other places that are handy. I know a busy businesswoman who keeps silence at home first thing every morning, but who also has discovered a recess in a building not far from work for an impromptu session of silence whenever she needs it. This break for silence can be surprisingly helpful. Just knowing that such a place exists can reduce stress.

Create a community of friends who keep silence with you.

Once you have developed some facility in silence keeping, practicing with others opens up entirely new vistas. You might form a small group—even just two or three people—who want to meet on a regular basis just to practice silence with you.

Visit a monastery.

Most monasteries practice some silence as part of their way of life, so they are wonderful places to experience a deep silence. There you will get the chance to learn from others who have practiced silence for many years, who have solved many of its problems and reaped many of its rewards. You will often find their group silence enormously supportive of your own efforts.

Locate a spiritual director.

As the desert monks realized, spiritual exploration without direction is not only potentially counterproductive, it can be downright dangerous. If you see a young monk attempting the ascent of the heavens without a guide, they advised, pull him down to the ground. A director can assist you in knowing which practices of silence are best for you at any given point in your spiritual journey, and when it might be useful to adjust your practices. The website for Spiritual Directors International (see *www.sdiworld.org*) can help you connect to a network of spiritual directors and locate one in your own area.

Resources for Further Study

The single indispensable element in the spiritual journey, say the Desert Fathers, is the spiritual director, or the soul friend. But as the poet W. H. Auden explained, books are our connection to the spiritual guides of the past, and they help us to resist the tyranny of the present moment. Even spirituality can be subject to trends and fashions.

I have tried here to present introductory work in many traditional Christian practices. A much older and decidedly dated, yet very detailed, manual covering some (but not all) of these is F. P. Harton, *Elements of the Spiritual Life* (Macmillan, 1932). Do not be put off by its density, its old-fashioned tone, or its rather elite spirituality. This volume still has much to offer.

The various forms of **sitting meditations** were developed mostly in monasteries during the first centuries of Christian history. A classic introduction to Christian monasticism at its origins is D. W. Chitty, *The Desert a City* (Oxford, 1966). The spirit of the early monks is best expressed in the *Sayings of the Desert Fathers*, available in several collections; one of the handiest of these is Thomas Merton's, recently (1994) reissued by Shambala in a tiny pocket edition as *The Wisdom of the Desert*. The *Sayings* also appear in *Western Asceticism* (Owen Chadwick, ed., *Library of Christian Classics*, 1958). For the larger historical context, the best introductions are Margaret Deanesley, *A History of Early Medieval Europe* (Methuen, 1960), and J. M. Wallace-Hadrill, *The Barbarian West* (2nd edition, Basil Blackwell, 1985).

Benedictine rumination is discussed by Dom Jean Leclercq in *The Love of Learning and the Desire for God* (Fordham, 1982). Sec also his article "The Benedictine Order" in the *New Catholic Ency-clopedia* (1967). The primary source is, of course, Benedict's *Rule*, available in a handy Image translation by Anthony C. Meisel and M. L. del Mastro (1975), as well as many other versions. The Rule does not give precise instructions for rumination, however; the technique developed as a response to the kind of reading suggested in the Rule.

Psalm repetition is described in the early fifth-century *Confer-ences* of John Cassian, which appear in *Western Asceticism*, men-tioned above. Cassian's task was, in a way, analogous to ours: He wanted to instruct the Western church in the ways of the Eastern solitaries, so that the former could translate their vigorous practices into their own circumstances. The method of psalm repetition is of a piece with the entire series of conversations he records, which show throughout the desire to integrate the elements of the Christ-ian life—to get prayer, meditation, corporate worship, study, work, and personal habits together into a unified expression of the Gospel.

Breath counting in a Christian context is explored by William Johnston in *Christian Zen* (Harper & Row, 1971). Aelred Graham's *Zen Catholicism* (Harcourt, Brace & World, 1963) explores the same subject in greater depth. For comparison, an older book, Ernest Wood's *Yoga* (Penguin, 1954) presents a quite comprehen-sive and thoughtful introduction to the practices of Hindu devotion for the Western reader. The classic account of the **Jesus Prayer** is in *The Way of a Pilgrim*, translated by R. M. French (Ballantine, 1974). Behind its theory and practice lie the great hesychast tradition, a monastic movement in later Patristic and medieval Orthodoxy that stressed keeping silence and practicing bodily stillness (the word hesychia is Greek for "silence" and "stillness"). *The Way of a Pilgrim* is, seen from one angle, the record of an experiment in bringing that tradition into the practice of a wandering layperson, neither ordained nor monastic, who is determined to bring the fruits of silence into his life and to practice unceasing prayer. A strong sam-pling of that tradition is provided by reading the following: 1) Ori-gen's most important work, the *De Principiis*, is available in the *New Advent* series of Patristic translations, which may be accessed through the Internet at www.newadvent.org; 2) The Cappadocian Fathers, Gregory of Nazianzus, Gregory of Nyssa, and Basil the Great, may be sampled in Edward Rochie Hardy's *Christology of the Later Fathers* (Westminster, 1954); 3) John of Damascus, whose *De fide orthodoxia* represents the classic systematic theology of the Eastern church, can be read in an older English translation by S.D.F. Salmon in the *Nicene and Post-Nicene Fathers* series (1899), available in many libraries.

Debra Farrington's recent *Unceasing Prayer: A Beginner's Guide* (Paraclete, 2002) is a 21st-century version of *The Way of a Pilgrim*—an extended response to St. Paul's admonition to "pray without ceasing." It may also provide a perfect complement to *Keeping Silence*, for though aimed at those who feel they have no time to pray formally, it offers useful suggestions for extending the silence of those who are able to keep silent time every day.

The *Spiritual Exercises* of **Ignatius Loyola** are translated by Anthony Mottula with an introduction by Robert Gleason (Image, 1964), as well as a variety of other translations.

The Stations of the Cross is a flexible tradition rather than a particular text. A balanced version is included in the Episcopal *Book of Occasional Services* (Church Hymnal Corporation, 1979). This version allows flexibility in the number of stations. Some scriptural purists have objected to the nonbiblical events in the traditional fourteen stations, so provision is made for a purely biblical version (omitting the stations, such as number 6, where a woman wipes the face of Jesus, or 13, where the crucified Christ is placed in Mary's arms). Similarly, it subordinates images to the texts—crosses are optional, or depictions of scenes—but it is quite clear that they are not essential to the exercise. Herbert van Zeller, a prolific and witty monastic author, considers the stations in his *Approach to Calvary* (Sheed and Ward, 1961). Raymond Chapman has also produced two books on the Stations of the Cross, suitable for use in Lent and Advent: *The Stations of the Nativity* (1999), and *The Stations of the Resurrection* (1999), both available from Morehouse Publishing.

Good secondary studies on the **Gothic church** (and, by extension, its modern counterpart) include Erwin Panofsky, *Gothic Art* *and Scholasticism* (Meridian, 1976), Emile Male, *Religious Art in France: The Thirteenth Century* (Princeton, 1984), and Henri Focillon, *The Art of the West in the Middle Ages,* vol. 1–2 (Cornell, 1980). An ingenious book, written at the popular level, is David Macaulay's *Cathedral: The Story of Its Construction* (Houghton Mifflin, 1973); a fine video version is also available. The kind of thought that inspired the art is very well expressed by Josef Pieper in his *Scholasticism;* a popular survey of the larger context of medieval thought is provided by Dom David Knowles in *The Evolution of Medieval Thought* (Vintage, 1962) or by C. S. Lewis in *The Discarded Image* (Cambridge University, 1964). More technical, but very worthwhile for those who find themselves spiritually in harmony with Gothic art, is Gordon Leff, *Medieval Thought* (Penguin, 1958). Since one important element in the design of the art was depicting the Bible, Beryl Smalley's *The Study of the Bible in the Middle Ages* (Notre Dame University, 1964) should also prove quite useful. But the best counterpart in words to the Gothic church building is the immense cathedral in words designed by the great scholastic theologians. The greatest of these, the *Summa* of St. Thomas Aquinas, is available in many abbreviated translations. A most accessible compilation is Paul Glenn's *A Tour of the Summa* (TAN Books, 1978), which presents the Summa in handy index form, eliminating the rich but complex dialectical format and leaving the content—a nice correlative to the visual organization of the Gothic church building.